WARRIOR

OF ZEN

WITHDRAWN

ALSO EDITED AND TRANSLATED
BY ARTHUR BRAVERMAN:

*Mud and Water: A Collection of Talks
by the Zen Master Bassui*

Edited, Translated, and
with an Introduction by
ARTHUR BRAVERMAN

WARRIOR
OF ZEN

The Diamond-hard
Wisdom Mind of
Suzuki Shōsan

Illustrations by
Hiroko Braverman

KODANSHA INTERNATIONAL
New York • Tokyo • London

LIBRARY
ST. LOUIS COMMUNITY COLLEGE
AT FLORISSANT VALLEY

For my parents

Kodansha America, Inc.
114 Fifth Avenue, New York, New York 10011, U.S.A.

Kodansha International Ltd.
17–14 Otowa I-chome, Bunkyo-ku, Tokyo 112, Japan

Published in 1994 by Kodansha America, Inc.
This is a Kodansha Globe original paperback.

Copyright © 1994 by Arthur Braverman
All rights reserved.

Printed in the United States of America

94   95   96   97   98   99   7   6   5   4   3   2   1

Library of Congress Cataloging-in-Publication Data

Warrior of Zen : the diamond-hard wisdom mind of Suzuki Shōsan / edited, trans-
lated, and with an introduction by
Arthur Braverman
illustrations by Hiroko Braverman.
p.   cm. — (Kodansha globe)
Includes bibliographical references and index.
ISBN 1–56836–031–2
1. Suzuki, Shōsan, 1579–1655.   2. Spiritual life—
Zen Buddhism.
I. Braverman, Arthur, 1942–   .   II. Braverman, Hiroko.
III. Suzuki, Shōsan, 1579–1655. Selections, 1994.   IV. Series.
BQ988.U889W37   1994
294.3'927—dc20   94—18320
                                                              CIP

Photographs in the section at the end of this book were provided
courtesy of Shigeo Suzuki.

Book design by Steven N. Stathakis
The text of this book was set in Garamond No. 3
Composed by Graphic Composition

The cover was printed by Phoenix Color Corporation,
Hagerstown, Maryland

Printed and bound by Arcata Graphics,
Fairfield, Pennsylvania

Contents

Acknowledgments

Supportive friends and family have always been a source of strength for me, but in this project in particular I have looked to them for technical help as well, and have not been disappointed. Thank you Jake Ainsworth, Ralph Edsell, Doug Honeyman, David Howard, Pico Iyer, Surya Dass Miller, and John Storm for reading the manuscript and offering many useful suggestions; thank you Mr. Shigeo Suzuki and Rev. Ichido Sato for showing me around Asuke and making available to me a wealth of literature and many wonderful photographs about Shōsan and his world; thank you Hiroko for your wonderful drawings, for being available to answer my many questions on the ambiguities of some of the passages, and for being, together with our daughter, Nao, patient and supportive of my work throughout this project; thank you Peter Haskel for your help with the editing and general advice (it's rare to have an editor so deeply knowledgeable of one's subject in such a specialized field); and finally, thank you Paul De Angelis and Kodansha for overseeing the project in such a caring manner.

Foreword

It is increasingly a commonplace that learning to live means, in large part, learning to die; that nothing measures our lives so firmly as our readiness to let go of them. The great Buddhist teachers have always turned a pitiless eye on the experience from which many of us would prefer to avert our gaze, seeing death as the ultimate—or an intermediate—challenge and adventure. Closer to home, a man of wise proportions such as Thoreau teaches us the virtue of deliberation, living each day, and approaching each encounter, as if it were our last.

The strength of Shōsan, the seventeenth-century warrior-turned-monk, is that he gives us a wake-up call about death so full-throated that it reverberates through the centuries. His voice coming through loud and clear in Arthur Braverman's wonderfully lucid and sensitive transmission, he carries himself like a two-fisted fighter, confronting death at every moment, and striding with his "warrior's glare" into the lion's den of death—or, more precisely, our fear of death. Death is famously a way of focusing our attention and sharpening our priorities: in Shōsan's disarming brand of "coward's Dharma," it also becomes a kind of samurai *zazen* that leads us back to a reality deeper than mere doctrine. Whenever students come to him with students' questions—what should we read, how should we study, whom should we ask—Shōsan's response is always bracingly decisive and direct: You should practice!

There is much else that this vigilant warrior can teach us, especially in a world that is ever more full of "strife and confusion." Over and over, he reminds us that Buddhism has nothing to do with gentle piety, or righteousness, or theory. It is only as strong as its usefulness in the marketplace. Over and over, he tells us that "public service is itself religious practice," and that "the World Dharma and the Buddha Dharma are one." Seclusion is not sanctity. Yet the soul of his teachings lies finally in his own example: standing upright, vital energies collected, with a clean sword in hand, ready to slash through distraction and delusion. Death, he reminds us, is the one experience that none of us can avoid, and the one battle that none of us can win. And to almost every question, he answers, in effect, "You will die! You will die!"

In the context of such muscular and unsentimental teaching, it is beautifully and supremely fitting that his words are here accompanied by Hiroko Braverman's delicate, and even feminine, rendering of the classic Oxherding Pictures, and of the *Niō* (guardian deities). They take us back to a wisdom that all traditions cherish (as Montaigne, Shōsan's contemporary, wrote, "He who has learned how to die has unlearned how to be a slave"). And they remind us of a no less important truth that concentrates the mind: to learn how to die, we must learn how to live.

—Pico Iyer
Nara
March 30, 1994

Introduction

Illustration on preceding page: The Niō.

From the beginning it's best to do zazen in the midst of strife and confusion. . . .

. . . What use can there be for a zazen requiring a quiet place? However appealing Buddhist teachings may be, the samurai should throw out anything he can't use when the moment for his battle cry arrives. So he never needs anything but the mind of the Niō *at all times. . . .*[1]

The *Niō* are the two guardian deities who stand on either side of the temple gate. Each carries a thunderbolt-like weapon (*kongōsho*) that, according to esoteric Buddhism, symbolizes the diamond-hard wisdom mind. Suzuki Shōsan, former warrior turned monk, seized upon the vital energy symbolized by these two ferocious-looking deities; he emphasized it to students, and demonstrated in his person the need to cultivate it in all activities. Because of its uniqueness, Shōsan became associated exclusively with his *Niō* zazen[2] as though it were the whole of his teaching. But *Niō* zazen was only one side of this very complex and distinctive Zen master and cannot be understood unless seen as an integral part of Shōsan's life and teaching.

Suzuki Shōsan was born at the end of an era that had seen Japan torn by civil war. Known as the Age of Warring States (1467–1568), it was a period when feudal lords of leading clans were contending for supremacy over the country. The warrior culture that pervaded Japan at this time had its roots in the seventh century when sons of the ruling aristocracy, having no posts in the capital, were sent to the provinces. There they administered and policed the provincial holdings of their families in the capital, while increasing their territory through warfare. Early chronicles testify to battles for domination of Japan by different races long before this period, but it was at this time that the seeds of the martial code, putting loyalty to one's lord and valor above all else, were planted.

By the twelfth century, when the leading warrior clans became the actual rulers of the country, they had adopted religions that complemented their martial ethic, rejecting others that were popular with their aristocratic predecessors. The democratic faith of Pure Land Buddhism, in which the aspirant could be saved by the sincere recitation of the name of the Buddha of Eternal Light, Amida, and the dynamic practice of Zen Buddhism, which stressed direct seeing into one's nature, replaced the esoteric Shingon and Tendai Buddhist sects.[3]

Pure Land Buddhism simplified religious practice by reducing it largely to the recitation of the name of Amida. That alone would allow the aspirant, upon his death, to enter the Western Paradise, one of the countless numbers of Buddha Lands. This simple faith-only approach to religion attracted many adherents, and Pure Land Buddhism spread widely among the masses, also attracting followers from the warrior class.[4]

Zen, with its rigorous discipline and meditation practice, attracted great numbers of warriors from the leading samurai clans. Because of its close connection with Chinese culture and its influence on the arts, Zen was adopted by the ruling families of the military governments from the thirteenth through the middle of the sixteenth century. One result of this government patronage of Zen was the growth of the *Gozan*, or Five Temple system, in the Rinzai School. The *Gozan* produced an impressive body of literature, but meditation practice seems to have taken a backseat to economic and institutional concerns.

Throughout the medieval period, teachers criticized the material prosperity of these official Zen institutions and the decadence that inevitably affected them. Dōgen Kigen (1200–1254), founder of the Sōtō Zen sect in Japan, left the capital and settled in Echizen Province, an area situated north of Kyoto that is known for its severely cold winters. In lectures compiled under the title *Zuimonki* (Record of Things Heard), he makes numerous references to the danger of putting prosperity before practice.

> When Zen Master Fang-hui of Mount Yang-chi[5] became abbot, the monastery was dilapidated, causing the monks many difficulties. One of the monks in charge suggested the building be repaired.
>
> Fang-hui said: "The buildings may be falling apart, but it is better than practicing on the ground or under a tree. If one section needs repair and the roof leaks, do zazen in a spot where it doesn't leak. If enlightenment came as a result of the construction of temple buildings, we would build them of gold and jewels. Enlightenment does not depend on the quality of the buildings; it depends on your zazen. . . ."
>
> . . . The Zen Master Lung-ya[6] said: "To study Buddhism you must first study poverty. Only then can you become intimate with the Way."
>
> From ancient times until the present, I've never heard of true students of the Way who possessed wealth.[7]

The Rinzai Masters Jakushitsu Genkō (1290–1367) and Bassui Tokushō (1327–1387) were two other dynamic Zen teachers who turned down appointments at the rich government-sponsored monasteries and held firm to their resolve to practice in accord with their understanding of the original intent of Zen. By the end of the fifteenth century, critics of the decline of true Zen practice grew fewer while temples grew richer and more corrupt. One figure stands out, however, for his biting criticism of the Zen world, the celebrated eccentric Ikkyū Sojun (1394–1481). Ikkyū not only wrote disapprovingly of the clergy but is said to have burned his certificate of enlightenment and walked around the capital demonstrating in a flamboyant manner how greed and hunger for power had squeezed the life out of Zen. In his poem "Rebuilding the Temple" he wrote:

A lifetime under the broken eaves of crumbling huts
Free from the vanities of glory and fame,
While in the temples greed and lust are made at home,
Long-neglected, the walls and roof of Yang-chi's house.[8]

The period from Ikkyū's death to Shōsan's birth spans most of the sixteenth century, a time when Zen practice had been so formalized that true Zen experience was rarely seen. By contrast, the seventeenth century marked a period of revival for Zen. Men like Shōsan, Shidō Munan (1603–1676), and Bankei Yōtaku (1622–1693) were rugged individualists who would settle for nothing less than the depth of experience that had characterized the Zen of antiquity. Shōsan, however, taught a personal blend of practices that is probably unique in the history of Zen. His method of zazen was truly his own, resembling none of the methods taught by past Zen Masters. His radical approach to the *nenbutsu* was unlike anything found in the writings of the Pure Land teachers. And his insistence on "death awareness," though certainly traceable to practices that have their inception in earlier Buddhism, was marked by an intensity and passion that was distinctly his own. Shōsan's personal and distinctive adaptation of these traditional practices must have puzzled and confounded many of his contemporaries.

How much this "radical" Zen can be traced to events in Shōsan's past is a matter of conjecture. However, his choice of such an active approach to meditation corresponds closely to the values dear to the samurai, and one wishes one knew more about the life of this former soldier before he took the tonsure.

Born into a warrior family in the province of Mikawa (present-day Aichi Prefecture) in 1579, Shōsan was raised during one of Japanese history's bloodiest periods. He was a direct retainer in the army of Tokugawa Ieyasu (1541–1616), who unified the war-ridden country and whose clan, the Tokugawas, would rule Japan for the next 250 years. Many scholars give Shōsan credit for having fought in the Battle of Sekigahara, the decisive battle in Ieyasu's campaign to unify Japan, but recently doubt has been raised as to whether Shōsan actually took part in the fighting.[9]

The eldest of five sons and two daughters, Shōsan came from an old samurai family. His brother Shigenari, the second oldest, and their father, Suzuki Shigetsu, fought alongside Shōsan in Ieyasu's campaigns, and his direct connection from childhood with Japan's most powerful military lord explains, to some degree, Shōsan's unquestioning loyalty to a government whose laws were rigidly regulating the Buddhist establishment.

Shōsan's biographer, Echū,[10] tells us of a dream his master's mother had of the Bodhisattva Fugen[11] entering her bosom before she gave birth to Shōsan, an omen not without precedent in Buddhist hagiography. In another entry, we learn that when Shōsan was four years old, a playmate died, and he asked where his companion had gone. Though not an unusual question for a child, it may be seen as a possible source of Shōsan's lifelong inquiry into death. This inquiry was to become a teaching tool, one so important as to induce him to say:

> Make the one character [ideogram] "death" master in your heart, observing it and letting go of everything else.[12]

At twelve years of age, Shōsan was adopted by a member of a seventy-man horse troop at Shioko in the province of Hitachi (present-day Ibaraki Prefecture). His brother Shigenari became the heir to the Suzuki family, and Shōsan remained close to him, fighting alongside Shigenari and Shigetsu in Ieyasu's final campaign.

Very little is known of Shōsan's family life, other than that he had a son and a daughter, and that his son was adopted by Shigenari. Nothing is known about his daughter or his wife. There is speculation, however, that he was married twice.[13]

During Shōsan's life as a warrior, he found time to visit teachers and develop his growing interest in Zen. He was probably born into the Jōdo sect, the leading religious organization in the Mikawa area and the sect of his lord Ieyasu. But while the flavor of Pure Land teachings was to remain with him throughout his life, Shōsan gravitated to Zen Buddhism.

Echū writes that Shōsan traveled extensively while still in the service of his Tokugawa lord, visiting various Zen masters. He mentions names such as Ryōson of Taho hermitage in Shimozuma, Motsuge of Erin monastery in Utsunomiya, Daigu and Gudō[14] of Myōshinji in Kyoto, and Shōsan's lifelong friend Ban'an (or Man'an) of Kiun monastery in Edo. Echū writes of Shōsan's ability to ask pointed questions and to cut through to the core of things, which he says encouraged these teachers to reassess their own understanding of Zen. Shōsan himself speaks of his natural ability to go right to the heart of a question:

> Saying things that cut through to the core is something I've always been strong at. When a subject is being discussed, I listen, quickly grasp its essence, and make a statement that cuts right through.[15]

It was at the request of Shōsan's lifelong friend, the Sōtō priest Ban'an, that in 1636 he composed *Fumoto no Kusawake* (Parting the Grasses at the Foot of the Mountain), an instructional manual for newly ordained monks. The manual explained the various practices handed down in Sōtō Zen tradition, although through the very personal understanding Shōsan brought to all Buddhist practices. Describing the purpose of the manual, Shōsan writes:

> One who seeks to practice the Buddha Way enters from the shallow to the deep. He must climb to the top of the mountain by parting the grasses at the foot. It is difficult to reach the top when one's practice is incomplete. To understand the meaning, you must set your sight on the methods handed down directly by the ancient masters. . . .[16]

This is followed by seventeen sections covering points that Shōsan felt were essential to training monks.

Ieyasu's victory at Osaka Castle in 1615 completed his control over the country. Shortly after this, Shōsan, whose duties may have been lightened, wrote his first pamphlet, *Mōanjō* (A Staff for the Blind), an attempt to demonstrate the superiority of Buddhism over Confucianism. There had been a growing feeling among the samurai that Confucianism, with its emphasis on living wisely in this world, was more valuable to Japan than Buddhism. Though Shōsan felt that Confucianism had its place in Japanese society, he believed that it should be considered subordinate to Buddhism, and that only then could it fulfill its true potential. Shōsan wrote *Mōanjō* to convince a fellow samurai of his error in believing that Confucianism was more useful than Buddhism. It was not long after that Shōsan made one of the most important decisions in his life—the decision to become a monk.

Shōsan decided to take the tonsure knowing full well that, as a samurai, such a step could incur the wrath of the reigning shōgun, Ieyasu's heir, Hidetada (r.1605–1623; d.1632). Shōsan could have been forced to commit ritual suicide and had his family line terminated. However, his resolve remained strong, and the shōgun took pity on him, perhaps as a result of Shōsan's past service in the army. In *Roankyō*, a record of Shōsan's discourses, he talks of his decision to become a monk and of some of the details surrounding the act. Though he tried to discourage others from taking the tonsure and always taught a form of secular Buddhism, this decision gave him the opportunity to concentrate on his own practice and to develop his unique teaching style.

In 1620, at age forty-one, Shōsan ordained himself. He first went to the Zen Master Daigu Sōchiku, perhaps to make his ordination official. According to Echū, Daigu refused to give him a new name because, in Daigu's words, Shōsan was already revered as a Buddhist teacher and a new religious name was not necessary. Others attribute Shōsan's keeping of his old name to his determination to respect secular Buddhism. At this time, Shōsan traveled through western Japan, visiting Buddhist holy places and Shinto shrines. He finally settled in Hōryūji in Nara to study the precepts of the Vinaya (Precepts) sect under a monk named Genshun Risshi, a Shingon (tantric) master from Mount Koya.[17] There he learned the fundamentals of primitive Buddhism not usually stressed in Zen temples in Japan. It was at Hōryūji that Shōsan was ordained a novice monk.

In 1623 Shōsan moved to Chidori Mountain in Mikawa. In *Roankyō*, he describes his life there:

> When I was engaged in Ritsu discipline on Chidori Mountain in the province of Mikawa, I lived on nothing but

barley gruel and boiled barley with rice. Because of the way I lived, my body was exposed to wind and rain, my stomach and intestines were affected by the raw food, and I became ill. My illness finally grew severe. Though I tried many different remedies, I was unable to make a complete recovery. All of the many doctors I saw simply gave up. I, too, thought I would die. . . .[18]

It was at this time that Shōsan broke one of the precepts that only a short while before he had vowed to uphold. In order to improve his physical condition to fight the illness that nearly took his life, Shōsan, following the advice of one of his brothers who was a doctor, ate meat. Shōsan remarks that he would have eaten the flesh of a corpse had he thought it would help, though he describes the act of eating meat as shameless.

In 1624, Shōsan moved to a hermitage known as Sekiheizan in Ishinotaira, a valley about twelve miles north of Okazaki Castle in Mikawa. According to Echū, it was a place of serene beauty, where monks and lay people from all over the country came to study with Shōsan. The Master, he said, brought joy to his listeners through his eloquent Dharma talks, and spent his evenings in the meditation hall practicing zazen.

Echū may have exaggerated Shōsan's popularity as well as the extent to which he was able to heal people and perform miracles. He writes of how Shōsan, through intensive sutra readings, put out fires on burial mounds and cured an ailing man. Though Shōsan himself rejected the idea that Buddhism was something that involved miracle-making, he did believe in the power of prayer and had a reputation as a healer. According to *Roankyō*, he performed sutra recitations to cure a lady who had threadlike worms coming out of her body.[19] From the record, however, we can see that Shōsan's interest in freeing his disciples from their mental delusions was far greater than any desire to be a physical healer.

Despite its beauty and serenity, and perhaps because of its isolation, Sekiheizan did not strike Shōsan as a place to settle permanently. He lived there for six years and then later returned for four years more, but his commitment was not to a life of seclusion. His calling was to spread the Dharma and to carry out a lifelong wish to convince the government to declare Buddhism—a Buddhism that transcended sectarian distinctions—the religion of the people. When asked about this wish, Shōsan responded:

> The true teachings of Buddhism cannot flourish without a directive from the government . . .
> Even if the Buddha were to appear in the world at this time, it would be difficult to establish the true teachings. With a government directive, however, the true teachings would immediately flourish. . . .[20]

This rather naïve faith in a government decree grew in part from Shōsan's warrior upbringing with its ideal of trust in one's lord, in Shōsan's case, the Tokugawa Shōgun. In addition, Shōsan felt that true Buddhism had long been dead in Japan and that as a monk it was his obligation to revive it.

> For more than two hundred years now, the true Dharma has been extinct in our country. . . .
> . . . Having received the Three Holy Treasures,[21] if you fail to share them with the people—and fail to make them a treasure of our land—you cannot call yourself a monk. . . .[22]

In many respects, Shōsan was a true product of traditional Japan and its feudal social values. He never doubted the validity of the four classes of people (samurai, farmers, artisans, and merchants), believed in exorcism and endorsed some seemingly bizarre healing practices. But his belief that Buddhism should have a significant influence on society as a whole, and that petty factional disputes within the Japanese Buddhist community drained its energy and hindered the true Way is very contemporary in flavor. His attitude toward women in both Buddhism and society, though not progressive by current standards, was, for his time, remarkably so.

Around 1632, Shōsan went to Osaka to visit his brother Shigenari, who held an administrative position in the Tokugawa government. Hearing that a local official was sentencing women to death simply for being family members of lawbreakers, he asked Shigenari to intervene on their behalf. This kind of act, Shōsan argued, violated Buddhist morality and was a cause of evil karma. Though an appeal of this nature to an oppressive military regime like the Tokugawa government subjected both Shigenari and Shōsan to accusations of disloyalty, Shigenari appealed several times, and eventually the death penalty was revoked. He then had statues of Amida Buddha and twenty-five bodhisattvas placed in a temple to aid the spirits of those who had already been put to death.

Shōsan spent most of his life as a monk teaching, traveling, and writing pamphlets on aspects of Buddhism. Though he himself had taken the tonsure, Shōsan stressed a kind of secular Buddhism. He was a reformer by nature, and it hurt him to see the true principles of Buddhism lost to greedy, power-hungry, and lazy clerics. He wanted the government to adopt what he regarded as "true Buddhism" in order to help put an end to the hypocrisy prevalent in the Buddhist temples, but was frustrated in his efforts to bring this message to Japan's rulers. Consistent with his belief in an integrated Buddhism, he generally discouraged people from entering the priesthood. "True Buddhism," he felt, should not be divorced from everyday life; it wasn't necessary to change your social status in order to experience the essence of the Buddha's teachings.

> According to the Buddha's words, "One who fully enters society lacks little from the Buddha world." This statement means that you can attain Buddhahood through the world's teaching. This is because the world's teaching is itself the Buddha Dharma. . . .
>
> . . . Unless you proceed according to the principle that you can attain Buddhahood through the world's teaching, you are completely oblivious to the intention of the Buddha. . . .[23]

After leaving Sekiheizan, Shōsan traveled to various monasteries throughout the country, teaching in his uncompromising manner—attacking corruption in the world and sloth in the temples. He was not very successful, according to Echū, and it is not difficult to understand why. The priests of these temples, one assumes, were hardly eager to hear of the sloth of the Buddhist clergy, especially from a relatively unknown preacher. Shōsan returned to Sekiheizan, but he made frequent trips to Edo (Tokyo); as time went on, he began to develop a following.

From 1642 to 1645, Shōsan settled in Higo (Kumamoto Prefecture) in Kyūshū where his brother Shigenari held an administrative post. Opposing the spread of Christianity in Japan, he convinced his brother of the need to build temples and propagate Buddhism. Receiving money from the government, Shōsan and his brother had thirty-two temples constructed, of which thirty-one were designated Sōtō Zen temples, the other being a Pure Land temple of the Jōdo sect. Tablets in honor of Ieyasu and Hidetada were placed in the Jōdo temple.

At this time, Shōsan wrote *Ha Kirishitan* (Christianity Refuted), a forcefully anti-Christian treatise. Shōsan's intolerance of Christianity may seem inconsistent with his belief that petty sectarian disputes were destroying Buddhism in Japan. Why couldn't Christianity be included in his grand scheme in the same way as Confucianism and Shinto? The first Christian missionaries entered Japan shortly after the arrival of Portuguese traders in the mid-sixteenth century. However, unlike followers of Confucianism and Shintō, whose religions were firmly established alongside Buddhism in Japanese tradition, the Christian fathers looked on all other religions as barbaric and hoped ultimately to destroy them. Though brilliant at adapting themselves to the customs of their host country, their ultimate object was to convert the Japanese to Christianity, and anything short of that they regarded as failure. Shōsan similarly objected to the Ikkō, or Jōdo Shin, sect of Buddhism[24] for its exclusiveness and its indifference to the Shintō shrines.

In 1648 Shōsan moved permanently to Edo, where he continued writing and teaching until shortly before his death. It was during this period that he wrote *Banmin Tokuyū* (The Meritorious Practice for All), assembled from a number of smaller pieces he had composed over the years. This was a treatise explaining how the four classes of Japanese society could transform their daily duties into "Buddha-work," and thus practice the Dharma in their natural callings.

Shōsan seems to have been something of a tragic figure in his final years, though he never gave in to disappointment. In 1653 he suffered the loss of his brother Shigenari. Protesting against the high taxes levied on the inhabitants of Higo, Shigenari had his request for lower assessments refused by a higher official and, following protocol, committed ritual suicide.[25] The next year Shōsan lost his close friend and spiritual companion, the priest Ban'an. But most disappointing for a teacher so passionate about Buddhism was the feeling that people did not listen to him. His expressed dream for the country to unite under the guidance of the "True Law" and for all the Buddhist sects to exist as one, fell upon deaf ears. Yet Shōsan apparently remained active and vibrant until the end. His life was one of ideals that never became realities and the reality of a teaching career so active as to be the ideal of many. In his last public statement, on his deathbed, refusing to give up hope, he asked a visiting samurai to plead with the government to consider his proposition for the revival of the true Dharma. Shortly after this request, Shōsan died peacefully on the twenty-fifth day of the sixth month of 1655. He was seventy-six years old and had been a monk for thirty-five years.

Several aspects of Shōsan's teachings stand out as particularly relevant to the world today: his insistence that Buddhism be meaningful to people in all walks of life, his assertion that it can be practiced in one's daily tasks, his use of "death awareness" as a means of arousing vital energy, and his injunction that, whatever the practice—zazen, *nenbutsu*, or mantra—it must be performed with the valorous spirit of the *Niō*.

Because of Shōsan's emphasis on a particular attitude toward practice rather than on any particular practice per se, it is easy to understand his reservations about recommending the tonsure to students. In his travels around the country after becoming a monk, he witnessed a great deal of corruption and lethargy among the clergy. For many of the monks he met, ordination was an escape from the insecurity of one world to the false security of another. Nothing was more contrary to Shōsan's vision of a new and energized Japanese Buddhism than the compromising attitude that typifies an indolent monastic system.

To each of the four social classes of feudal Japan, Shōsan demonstrated a way to practice that would allow it to fulfill its vital role in the social order. To each group he pointed out that if their daily work was performed in the proper spirit, they were doing Buddha's work. To farmers, he said:

> Farming is itself a Buddhist activity. There is no need to seek practice elsewhere. Your body is the Buddha body, your mind the Buddha mind, and your work the work of the Buddha. . . .
> If you cultivate the land, reciting *Namu Amida Butsu* with ev-

ery movement of the hoe, you will surely reach Buddhahood. Just leave everything to Providence, be honest, and do not arouse personal desires. . . .[26]

The value of their work, Shōsan told the farmers, was shown by the fact that heaven had entrusted to them the nourishing of the world. When they persevered in their work, painfully hard as it might be, their minds were clear and unvexed, and so, in essence, they were doing Buddha's work all the time.

To artisans, Shōsan taught that all trades are Buddha practice and that Buddhahood could be attained through their sincere work as craftsmen. Though everyone possesses Buddha-nature, people unaware of this fact stray from the Buddha Way and become deluded ordinary beings. So people need no special practice other than the performance of their trade with a firm faith in their own Buddha-nature.

Merchants, regarded with suspicion in feudal Japan, occupied the lowest rung of the social ladder, even while the need for their services, and hence their actual importance, was growing rapidly. Shōsan managed to formulate a Buddhist ethic for these merchants, giving them the spiritual guidance needed in their profession. Shōsan does not discourage merchants from making a profit; in fact, he tells them that their profits will be high, a reward from the heavens, if they trade without greed or clinging. But he adds that if they despise their wealth, a great faith will rise in them, and enlightenment will emerge through a constant unshakable meditation derived from this faith.

Shōsan, a samurai until shaving his head in his forty-first year, counseled many sons of samurai. He found little difficulty in dealing with the apparent contradiction of his own decision to become a monk and his recommendation that other samurai not give up their profession to do the same. One reason was the lethargy he found in so many of the temples he visited in his travels around the country. More convincing still, however, was his own experience of living in seclusion in the mountains, a life he eventually abandoned to live in intimacy with the masses.

Years ago, I loved living in the mountains. If I saw a small forest, I wanted to build a retreat there, and I did live in the mountains on occasion. But it wasn't written in the stars, so I didn't end up there. Yet things have worked out fine. Had I lived in that manner, I would have become a good Buddhist while never understanding my faults. The fact that I had thought previously that living in the mountains was a good thing and now feel it not to be good is, I believe, a result of advancing in my practice.[27]

It was this false understanding of the "good Buddhist" that Shōsan saw as a danger to the true religious life. If the "good" Buddhist was one who shaved his head and lived in seclusion, rarely mixing with the people of the world, where was the Buddhist compassion for all sentient beings? This artificial distinction between the sacred recluse and the worldly commoner led Shōsan to declare the Buddhist teachings and the teachings of the World to be one.

> The World Dharma is the same as the Buddha Dharma. If you do not have faith that you can attain enlightenment through the World Dharma, you know nothing of the true essence of Buddhism. . . .[28]

Shōsan told samurai that both Dharmas established morality and uprightness, reminding them that they had the opportunity to develop these virtues through service to their lord. The courage they cultivated in this service, he added, was a prerequisite to entering the Buddha Way. This courage may wane and be replaced by fear as death approaches; so they shouldn't think that they are free of fear just because they are not aware of its presence. But as samurai, he told them, they should be grateful for a life that allows them the opportunity to see their fears. For Shōsan, the warrior's profession demands the most important qualities possessed by a seeker of Buddhism: energy, courage, and an awareness of imminent death:

> Put everything aside and only study death. Always study death, free yourself from it, and when death actually comes, you won't be flustered. . . .[29]

Shōsan's emphasis on "studying death" (*shi ni narau*) is hardly surprising given his samurai background. Such practice is stressed in records of samurai leaders throughout this period. The celebrated chieftain Takeda Shingen (1521–1573), for example, counsels:

> The practice of Zen has no secret, except standing on the verge of life and death. . . .[30]

In Shōsan's case, however, the practice of death awareness has its roots in a personal battle to grasp death's meaning, and this personal element adds another dimension to his practice:

> From the beginning, my character has been such that I cannot forget about death. Wherever I am, I can never let my guard down. I surpass others only in my aversion to death. That's why I practice with the warrior's glare. Actually, it is because of my cowardice that I have come this far. . . .[31]

For Shōsan, it was not simply a matter of overcoming the fear of death. He was conscious of his fear, and his practice evolved from this awareness. The awareness of death was, for him, real living. He felt that the promise of enlightenment or of rebirth in the Pure Land kept the practitioner from living here and now.

The reported experiences of many terminally ill patients closely resemble Shōsan's description of the awareness of imminent death. Shōsan points out that we are all terminal patients, most of us in a constant state of denial. Many patients, informed that their illness is terminal, respond similarly: "This isn't happening to me, it can't. . . ." Some die never getting beyond this stage, while others begin to face the reality of their situation. In the process, they report, there are periods of fearing the unknown and periods of accepting it. The fear is sometimes described as an existential doubting, not unlike the "great doubt" referred to by Zen masters. And like the "great doubt" it leads to a great opening, an acceptance of what *is*, when the patient doesn't try to run from it. But this is usually not a simple process of proceeding from A to B with no backsliding. For most, there is fluctuation between fear and acceptance, between holding on and letting go. Shōsan's experience seems to bear this out. He talks of his bondage and of his experiences of freedom, confessing at one point that "though I've practiced until my eightieth year, I'm still not free";[32] and a moment later referring to a time when "you could have threatened to cut off my head and it wouldn't have meant a thing to me."[33]

Shōsan, like other Buddhist teachers, saw the source of human suffering in attachment to a personal "I." His own experience, however, taught him that this "I" was not something he could simply throw out and have done with. For Shōsan, the attachment to a personal "I" manifests itself in the fear of death, a fear from which he never completely freed himself. Shōsan describes the practice of "studying death" as the most suitable for him, and it played a major part in his teaching. But here, too, he does not think of death as something one resolves to study and quickly conquer. He seems to ask his students to assume an attitude of constantly confronting death, never assuming the matter is settled. Responding to a question about the essentials of Buddhism, Shōsan remarks: "I don't know anything I can teach you." But a moment later, he adds unexpectedly: "You will die! You will die! Recite the *nenbutsu*. Never forget death!"[34] And on another occasion urges: "Make the one [Chinese] character 'death' the master in your heart, observing it and letting go of everything else."[35]

Throughout Zen's history, kōan[36] training has been a part of Zen tradition in both Sōtō and Rinzai schools, though people today often associate it with the Rinzai sect.[37] It is not clear whether Shōsan used kōans in the traditional way with his students, but he discusses and interprets them throughout Part II of *Roankyō*. When questioned about the relative value of kōan practice and "guarding death" (*shi o mamoru*),[38] Shōsan insists that kōan practice is superior. But he adds that studying death is more suitable for him, implying that studying death is more suitable for beginners, those not yet ready to practice the meditation of the Buddha. It is Shōsan's inclusion of himself that adds to the element of true inquiry in these encounters where student and teacher together seek the truth.

It is not hard to understand why Shōsan preferred the practice of guarding death to study of the more abstract kōans. He was skeptical of "cleverness," particularly the kind used by many of the young monks he encountered to cover up a lack of true understanding.

> If you practice speaking, you can talk about anything. Buddhists today think that clever arguments are fine, and others respect them for being adept at this kind of talk. Actually, there isn't anything more useless than clever arguments. . . . When I was young, I, too, made a great mistake here. I often fell into clever argumentation.[39]

Because he was more at home speaking to simple folk than to learned priests or intellectuals, the tangible nature of the concept of death awareness appealed to Shōsan. It was easier for ordinary people to grasp this concept; hence, he found it a more suitable practice than *nenbutsu* study. Wanting people to feel the immediacy of impermanence and the need to practice in this very moment, he chose a subject that all were familiar with: death.

Shōsan sees enlightenment as something that requires concerted effort over many lifetimes. True enlightenment, the enlightenment of the Buddha, is something that Shōsan has seen but cannot yet call his own. Quick certification of monks who have *kenshō*, an enlightenment experience, he warns, is a mistake. He says he threw out his own *kenshō* because it didn't suit him, and he refers to it as a passing state of mind that allowed him to "dance with gratitude" and "feel no concern even if his head were cut off," but eventually left him in his old state of attachment to the body.[40]

Enlightenment, Shōsan says, is "a mind that contemplates impermanence," and he insists that it requires a tremendous amount of energy, exerted constantly. Uninterrupted contemplation of death will keep your *ki* (vital energy) roused and sharpen your state of awareness. When you are attentive, you will see the importance of guarding against the demons of various delusions, who are always ready to take control of mind and body. Shōsan likens this to a block of doubt (*ikko gidan*). It requires tremendous energy to carry this doubt. Similarly, it requires tremendous energy to carry the seed of enlightenment. But this is still not complete enlightenment. This seed must be carried through numerous lifetimes before it will sprout into the enlightenment of the Buddha. An occasional *kenshō* and the recognition one receives for it are, for Shōsan, among the reasons for the sorry state of Buddhism.

Though Shōsan himself never reached this state of enlightenment, or met or read of anyone, apart from the Buddha, who did, he believed in its possibility. Though you may not carry the hope of enlightenment in this life, he said, if you see the need to practice through countless lives (which he referred to as carrying the seed), you will exert yourself every moment and so keep your practice pure. Then you won't fall into the trap of waiting for enlightenment to happen, the surest way to let your energy wane.

This, for Shōsan, is the *Niō* spirit: making effort from moment to moment. The *Niō* do not practice vigorously with the object of becoming Buddhas. Vigorous practice is their nature; they see delusion everywhere and guard against its attack.

While Shōsan laments his own lingering attachment to the body, it is his keen awareness of his limitations that makes him a model of the kind of Buddhist practice he espouses. Lingering attachments drain your energy if you don't make efforts to guard against them. For Shōsan, keeping up your energy is always the way to practice. One can do this through recitation of the *nenbutsu*, sitting in meditation, cultivating the earth, selling one's wares, or preparing for war, so long as these acts are performed with a mind aware of the impermanence of all things. The urgency generated by this awareness adds life to one's practice, a life that Shōsan demonstrated in his person and held to be essential to waking Buddhism from its stupor.

The selections in this book are drawn from *Roankyō* (Donkey-Saddle Bridge), a collection of Shōsan's talks in three parts, recorded by his disciple Echū. Written in a colloquial style of Japanese spoken in Shōsan's period, the text records talks that Shōsan delivered at various times during his teaching career. Echū combined discourses that other disciples had recorded, either as verbatim notes or from memory, with his own notes and recollections.

In *Roankyō* we find Shōsan reflecting on his own life and discussing incidents that were crucial in forming his unique and highly personal approach to Zen. Because of its distinctive, spontaneous character, Shōsan seems more vibrant in *Roankyō* than in any of his other works.

Echū took the work's title from the story of an attendant who went to the battlefield where his lord had been killed in order to bring back his remains. Thinking he had found a piece of the master's jawbone, he brought back a bit of wood from a saddle—Echū's humble way of saying that he could never capture the true spirit of his teacher.

A notable feature in this record is Shōsan's lack of concern for how he appears to the world at large. He does not fret that the advice he gives one student may not be philosophically consistent with that given another. When he responds to a questioner, he deals with that person alone, always giving everything he's got. When you read his words, you feel that you are touching a human being, passionate, outspoken, and honest.

Translator's Note

Roankyō is divided into two parts. The selections in Part 1 have the flavor of informal talks. These sections are most lively and make up the greater part of the translation. I have also included in Part 1 selections of Shōsan's personal reflections, which comprise a major source of biographical information about him.

Shōsan's commentaries on traditional Zen topics and his vision of a new Japanese Buddhism comprise Part 2, a much shorter section, which is important for a fuller picture of the man and his teaching.

In most cases, sections from the original Japanese text were taken in their entirety. When material was omitted, I have indicated it with ellipses. The captions at the head of each section are mine, none appear in the original. *Roankyō* does not seem to be arranged in any special order though the latter sections are of Shōsan's final days. I have taken liberties in rearranging some sections where I felt they would be relevant to sections that preceded or followed. The page numbers at the end of each section refer to Shōsan's original Japanese text. To sections where clarification of some point seemed helpful, I have added commentary. The commentary is in italics and is separated from the text by ellipses of three asterisks.

A short glossary of important Buddhist terms that appear in the introduction and text with which some readers might not be familiar has been included. The Japanese form of a glossary term is listed first when it appeared that way in the text.

—Arthur Braverman
Ojai, California
February, 1994

Warrior of Zen

Illustration on preceding page: Fudo Myō-ō (Sanskrit: Acala; The Immovable).

1

*Unorthodox
Zen*

Become a Vengeful Spirit of the Buddha Dharma

One day the Master said: "Nowadays people no longer talk of the daring, immovable force of the Buddha Dharma. Though with regard to gentility, piety, and unselfishness, people have improved, no one has honed his vital energy like a Vengeful Spirit.[1] Hone your fearless mind and become a Vengeful Spirit of the Buddha Dharma." *(p. 138)*[2]

* * *

Ki, translated here as vital energy, plays a central role in Shōsan's teaching. It implies, for him, a movement in the body of a basic spiritual force that can be called upon when one gives total attention to the present moment. This energy, according to Shōsan, is employed naturally by samurai in the midst of battle, and should be summoned by Buddhist practitioners throughout their daily lives. As long as the level of this energy remains high, Shōsan declares, one will not be overwhelmed by deluded thoughts.

I know nothing about piety or enlightenment

The Master said: "To practice the Buddha Dharma, you should model yourselves after Buddhist images. But beginners should not focus on the image of the *Tathagata*³ (*Nyorai*), for they are not yet able to do *Tathagata* zazen. They should simply focus on the *Niō* and *Fudō*⁴ and do *Niō* zazen. Initially, think of the *Niō* as the entrance to the Buddha Dharma and of *Fudō* as the first of the Buddhas. That's why the *Niō* stand at the gate and *Fudō* is the first of the thirteen Buddhas. If you don't acquire this vital energy, you'll succumb to delusion. You need only apply yourself single-mindedly with a strong spirit. But nowadays the Buddha Dharma has declined, and there aren't any good methods. No one makes use of his vital energy. There are only dead people. In the Buddha Way, however, it is the living who make use of their vital energy. Unaware of this, some become gentle, pious, and withdrawn, thinking that this is the Buddha Dharma. Others walk around deranged, their noses in the air, entertaining the meaningless notion that they are enlightened. I know nothing about either piety or enlightenment. Twenty-four hours a day with my buoyant mind⁵ I am engaged in conquering all things. Having acquired this unwavering energy of the *Niō* and *Fudō*, all of you should practice so you will overcome the deluded thoughts arising from bad karma."

Then the Master opened his eyes widely, clenched his fists, gritted his teeth, and said: "When you guard yourself firmly and confidently, no one will be able to impose anything upon you. With this one daring, vital energy, your practice will be complete. You need nothing else. If you let your guard down, whatever the practice, it won't work. Firmly fix your gaze and practice zazen." {pp. 138–139}

Practice imitating Buddhist images

One day the Master said: "In practicing the Buddha Way, the only important thing is the acquisition and use of the vast, unwavering energy of the *Niō* and *Fudō*. To push the body-mind to the brink is the only Buddhism I know. If you want to follow my approach to Buddhist practice, rouse your vital energy, fix your gaze, and acquire the energy of the demon-conquering forms of *Niō* and *Fudō*. Guarding this *Niō*-mind, you will overcome the delusion created by evil karma. I've never heard of anyone since antiquity who has practiced imitating Buddhist images like this. Yet it suits me, and frees me in all my activities. You find mention of the daring zeal of the Buddha in various sutras. Without acquiring this vital energy, you will never overcome delusion. You must realize that acquiring the energy of the Buddhist images is your most urgent concern. If you lack vitality, there will be no transfer of this vital energy. So fix your attention solely on the Buddhist images and follow your *vajra* (diamond) mind[6] day and night."{*p. 139*}

Only others will die

One day, after a funeral, the Master said in astonishment: "People think that only others will die. They forget that sooner or later they will, too. They carry on without so much as a thought that death could possibly happen to them. Then they're shocked when it comes upon them unexpectedly. How foolish!" {*p. 144*}

If you try for quick results, you'll only regress

One day someone asked about Buddhahood. The Master responded:

"What we call Buddhahood is the fact that all things are originally empty. Fundamentally, there is no me, no you, no Dharma, no Buddha. Buddhahood is complete separation from everything, letting go and being free. Whether it is satori or anything else, if something is there, *it* is not. Kōans like 'the old lady burning the hut'[7] testify to this."

Again the Master said: "It is unnecessary for those with little free time to come here regularly. Whatever I have to say, I've written in *Tokuyū* (Meritorious Way of Life) and *Kusawake* (Parting of the Grasses).[8] I have nothing to say beyond that. You should examine those works carefully."

The questioner said: "I have engaged in a fair amount of religious practice but have made no progress."

The Master responded: "It's not an easy matter. If it were that easy, I would be an arhat[9] or a bodhisattva. But I still haven't left the world of hungry ghosts and fighting demons. That's why, more and more, I engage in severe practices. Even if you apply yourself once as though you were brushing fire from your head, it will be of no avail if you don't continue. If you try for quick results, you'll only regress." {*p. 145*}

A precious story

One day someone came and said: "When the wife of a certain lord had to defecate, she said it was so dreadful to have someone clean it up that she would pay the man who cleaned the toilet some money."

Hearing this, the Master exclaimed: "What a grateful person! How wonderful! If I were to live with a group of people, I would want us all to take turns cleaning the toilets. It's not good for those placing their hopes in the next world [i.e., wanting to be born in the Pure Land] to use people even to clean their toilets. That was a truly splendid thing I just heard. It reminds me of an ancient story. A learned man once spent the night in a certain mountain temple. The following day, on seeing a twelve- or thirteen-year-old novice, he said: 'Last night this boy had the mark of one who would die within three days; but this morning he has the mark of one who will live a long life of some eighty years. How strange that his life expectancy should have increased by seventy years in one evening!' He asked what virtuous thoughts had arisen in the novice and what virtuous deeds he had performed. All the people of the temple were shocked. They asked the boy to recount the particulars of his experience. The novice said: 'I know of no good deeds that I have done. However, when I went to the toilet last night, the stepping board was stained, and it was difficult to endure being there even for a little while. At that time, the thought came to me that while I find it difficult to be here even for a moment, my mother used to be covered all over with my feces and hadn't a thought of discomfort. She thought only of how dear I was to her. I thought, alas, how difficult it is to repay such a deep favor! And with the intention of trying to repay it, I wiped the toilet board clean with my own hand. I don't remember doing anything else.' Everyone was moved by such virtue. Isn't this a precious story?" {p. 148}

Rouse death-energy

In the spring of the fourth year of Keian (1651), the Master said: "Rather than carrying around your own views, it's better to rouse death-energy.[10] From the time I was quite young, I had an inkling of this vital energy, but it wasn't until a long time after that it was transformed to death-

energy. I adopt the mind of one about to have his throat cut, just as if my own throat were about to be cut. When I hear of all the people who die, I receive death's vital energy just like that. I don't know how much of what I am saying has penetrated your hearts. When I'm attacked by the anguish of death, my heart pounds and it's quite unbearable. As time passes, I should find myself drained of this vital energy, and yet I never seem to be without it. At first I thought it was harmful, but later I realized that this energy is the perfect medicine for any disease. It takes care of everything. It even shows me how to reason. One who possesses this death-confronting energy will gradually improve. So I believe this death-energy can be the beginning of freedom from birth and death."
{p. 149}

Zazen in the midst of strife and confusion

One day the Master instructed a certain samurai: "From the beginning, it's best to do zazen in the midst of strife and confusion. A samurai, in particular, must be able to do zazen while uttering his battle cry. Guns are firing, lances are flying, and amidst the confusion, you send up a battle cry. It's here that you can clearly make good use of your practice. What use can you have for the sort of zazen that needs a quiet place? However appealing the Buddha Dharma may be, the samurai should throw out anything he can't use when the moment for his battle cry arrives. So he never needs anything but the mind of the *Niō*. Other than this mind of the *Niō*, none of the myriad things is of any use to beginners."

The Master added: "All the arts, including war, are produced with the energy from meditation. The art of war cannot develop if the mind is slack." He then mimicked someone holding a sword at the ready position and said: "This energy of meditation is everything. However, the warrior meditates only when he is performing his duty. As soon as he puts aside his sword, he relaxes his attention. A Buddhist practitioner, on the other hand, always uses this energy, never relaxes it. That's why he is never defeated. He practices gradually, building up fervor, and as in Noh[11] singing or in clapping to a beat, he harmonizes with everything and perfects all virtue. That is the kind of activity I call Buddha Dharma." {p. 171}

Kill the mind

One day someone came and said: "My ancestors have hunted birds for generations. Unless I continue doing this kind of work, I'll starve. Please teach me how to attain Buddhahood while continuing in my work."

The Master responded: "Know that it's your mind that will fall into hell. Each time you kill a bird, seize the mind and kill it. If you kill your whole mind, you'll attain Buddhahood." *{pp. 185–186}*

The buoyant mind

One day someone asked: "How can I use the 'buoyant' mind[12] you wrote about in *Shimin Nichiyō*[13] (Daily Activities of the Four Classes)?

The Master said: "The buoyant mind is the mind that longs to enter the lion's den. It is the mind that presses on, little by little, resolving to fight to the death. Without such vital energy, you will not be able to make use of this mind in different situations. Maintaining this vital energy in order to detach yourself from life and death is the beginning and end of Buddhist practice. If you detach yourself from life and death, you will attain Buddhahood. So it's solely through this vital energy that we realize Buddhahood. Nothing else is needed. Your personal understanding is of little use. Just as poison can be used as medicine, medicine can become poison. Often your personal understanding turns out to be your enemy. Rather than cultivating this personal understanding, rather than cultivating *anything*, it is better just to train with an uncompromising mind. An old song says: 'Satori that is unrealized is true satori. A realized satori is satori in a dream.' Indeed, a realized satori is dangerous. I prefer satori that is unrealized. The *Nenbutsu Ōjō* [entering the Pure Land through chanting the *nenbutsu*] of Hōnen[14] and other Pure Land teachers is an unrealized satori." *{p. 236}*

* * *

Shōsan appears here once more to be attacking the "certified kenshō*" that was so much a part of the Zen establishment. For Shōsan, this* kenshō *brought with it a pride in one's accomplishment that was more harmful to the student than the benefit of the* kenshō *itself. Like other reformers of this period, he preferred the simple, selfless faith-mind of the peasant who acted out of enlightenment without any awareness of it.*

Become a monk and you'll create hell

The son of a vassal of the shōgun arrived, asking to be ordained. The Master said: "Fundamentally speaking, I disapprove of your quitting your profession and seeking the Buddha Dharma. To renounce your position as a samurai shows a lack of vitality. As a religious practice, nothing surpasses public service. Become a monk and, to the contrary, you'll create hell. Public service is itself religious practice."

The Master repeated this over and over. However, the vassal's son was determined to realize his heart's desire, and refusing to listen, pressed his wish to be ordained.

The Master said: "If that's the case, there's nothing I can do about it. It's entirely in your own hands. As a rule, we don't ordain monks at my place, but you can have your head shaved anywhere. But putting that aside for the moment, don't get stuck later on. Listen to what I have to say now. When the government officials come to inquire, simply reply: 'I have nothing to say other than the fact that I am withdrawing because I hate this world. If this is thought to be unlawful, punish me.' After making your statement, present yourself to them. If you are prepared to cut open your belly,[15] you can shave your head. This is one point. Another point is that though you become a monk, you still require food, clothing, footwear, and tissues. Allow at least three gold pieces *(ryō)* a year. Don't shave your head without giving thought to this, later becoming a hungry ghost. But if you do understand this, go ahead and shave your head. It's also a mistake to take charge of a temple and eat the precious alms offered by donors. And it would be shameful to depend on a relative who can barely get on in the world himself. It would be better to lay down your life for your Master, receiving food from the government. As a rule, don't receive favors. Live by your own means. That's another point. If you understand all these things, do as you please. But don't get stuck later on."

The samurai responded: "How can I get stuck so long as I give up my body for the sake of the Dharma?"

The Master said: "Throwing away your body indiscriminately cannot be called Buddhism. If that is Buddhahood, find someone and have him cut off your head! Is plunging to your death in a river or a moat attaining Buddhahood? Throwing away your body means giving up attachments. So long as you give up attachments, though you still have a body, it is no longer an obstruction. This doesn't mean, however, that you can let the body go idle. It also goes without saying that it's wrong to work the body until you become sick.

"Do you really think that you throw away your body when you shave your head? On the contrary, shaving your head is seeking comfort for your body. When you make a vow to be reborn in the Pure Land, isn't that for the sake of your body? If you are throwing away your body, why aren't you doing so in the service of your present lord? There is no better way of giving up your body than doing something you dislike. Since a strong mind is an essential factor in religious practice, a samurai enjoys a more suitable position than a monk. The reason is that a samurai, having a lord, cannot afford to be careless. He must have the energy to draw his long or short sword[16] and advance with a shout. You lack even this level of energy. How on earth can there be any value in becoming a monk and letting your energy wane?"

The samurai asked: "Regardless of whether one is a monk or a layman, what is religious practice?"

The Master instructed: "Religious practice means firmly arousing the mind that vows to detach itself from life and death; not losing sight of this concentrated mind even if you sink to the lowest pits of hell; and vigorously maintaining this mind while it passes through countless incarnations, finally liberating itself from life and death. You must strengthen this mind far more than your ordinary mind. If you guard your mind in this manner, you are a man of unyielding faith and a practitioner. Is your own aspiring mind of this nature?"

The samurai said: "I do not aspire to the Way to that extent. Because I am easily swayed by things around me, I feel I should start by moving away from Edo for at least ten years."

The Master responded: "With that kind of mind, you could never be said to aspire to the Way. I've never known feelings of sadness or annoyance to obstruct me." He added: "In order to reveal [your mind],[17] you should express what you've realized in detail."

The samurai said: "I've realized the teaching that the five aggregates (form, sense-perception, thought, confection, and consciousness) are all empty."

The Master said: "That is the mind of the ancients, not *your* mind.

No matter how much you employ the words of great sages, trying to make them your own, how can an ordinary person like you ever make real use of them? When you reach the essence of fundamental emptiness, you will be able to put it into practice. You think of everything as truly existing, don't you? Let me tell you this: Throw out everything you have learned, all your delusions about Buddhism, and chant the *nenbutsu*."

The samurai said: "After I practiced zazen for a while, light appeared before me. When I reported this to the Elder Mutoku,[18] he said it was the light of the Dharma-body,[19] and that if I exerted myself more and more, my whole body would be filled with light. I thought that I would become ordained and cultivate this practice for a sustained period."

The Master said: "You have made a great mistake. That light often appears because one's vital energy is withering. If you treat it as something worthwhile, you will eventually go crazy. Haven't you noticed a drop in your energy level?"

The samurai responded: "Yes, it has dropped quite a bit. The sound of something being ground in an earthenware mortar echoes in my chest until I can hardly bear it."

The Master said: "Look at that! See how you've lost significant energy? You still have valuable time left. Quickly discard this practice. That Mutoku fellow is dangerous. I have heard about him. Recently news reached me of an eighteen- or nineteen-year-old Rinzai monk whom Mutoku revered as one who had seen into his own nature. If being enlightened were that simple, I, too, would be a Buddha or a bodhisattva. When I was young, I made up my mind to realize the great matter, arousing the desire for enlightenment till it was like a flame burning in my heart. And though I've practiced until my eightieth year, I'm still not free. If Mutoku can revere such people, his Buddhism is clear to me. Nowadays there are many teachers like him. Though young practitioners may have some understanding, I can't revere them. Religious practice is not something you can easily become passionate about. This much I clearly realized. When I saw how in the *Hōbutsu Shū* (Treasure Collection)[20] the phrase 'Everything is impermanent' caused Sessen Dōji[21] to prepare to give up his life, the meaning of the phrase 'Everything is impermanent' clearly came home to me. Then, in my sixtieth year, one morning at around four o'clock, the meaning of the Buddha considering all the people of the three worlds as his children[22] became clear to me. In fact, at this time, even when I saw ants, I thought, 'How sad their lives, full of pleasure and pain!' and the urge to find a means to save them penetrated to my marrow. That feeling lasted three days and was gone. Yet I still feel some benefit from it. From that time on, I have been able to arouse this compassionate mind to some degree.

"*Kenshō* (seeing into one's own nature), too, is something I have experienced. From the twenty-seventieth to the twenty-eighth day of the eighth month of my sixty-first year, I felt completely detached from life and death and in touch with my true nature. I danced with gratitude, feeling that nothing existed. At that time, you could have threatened to cut off my head and it wouldn't have meant a thing. Yet after thirty days like this, I decided it didn't suit me. It was nothing more than a realization based on a particular state of mind. So I discarded it and returned to my previous state. I filled my heart with death and practiced uncompromisingly. As I might have known, it had all been a big delusion. And here I am now, treasuring this bag of manure called Shōsan.

"Sometime later, I was similarly transformed as I realized the spirit of Fuke's[23] mind during a short walk of a few hundred yards. This was very beneficial to me. I wanted to practice through many lives with a vigor as great as Fuke's. I realized that Fuke was without a doubt a man of the Buddha realms. That Kayō, Mokuto[24] and Rinzai[25] were, respectively, dubbed a new bride, a granny, and a young servant made sense to me. From Fuke's perspective, they were all blind children. Though one has experienced *kenshō*, he may still have blind spots. What's more, though I practiced hard enough to have experienced various transformations, then threw out all those experiences and returned to my original state of continual practice, I still prize this bag of manure. Become a monk yourself now and practice until you are eighty years old and see what happens. You will not change at all. So long as you realize that you are crazy[26] whether or not you shave your head, go ahead and shave it. But if you think that shaving your head will improve you, you are making a big mistake. If you do change, it will be because you have become possessed or mad."

After a pause, the samurai said: "Having felt this strongly till now, wouldn't I look odd if I didn't follow through and become ordained?"

The Master responded: "What you said before isn't something that you can't go back on. If, afterward, you decide to return to lay life, do it—even if it means becoming a common foot soldier. It is an indication that your mind is unclear if you wonder what someone might say should you become such and such a person in the future.

"When I was in my forties, I became intensely disgusted with this world. When an official came to inquire, I said that I could no longer live in society this way, and that if that were considered wrong, I should be punished. I then withdrew, and, preparing to commit suicide, suddenly shaved my head. This was reported to the attendant [a military officer] and to the shōgun's counselor, and they were asked to inform his lordship that Suzuki Kudayū [i.e., Shōsan] had gone mad. But the counselor took pity on me. 'Well, now,' he considered, 'what a strange report! How can I mediate properly if I say that someone who is quite sane is mad?' He then waited for an opportunity, and when the shōgun was in good humor, he remarked during a casual evening conversation: 'Suzuki Kudayū has suddenly conceived the desire to practice the Way.' How did the shōgun take this? With a deep compassion drawn from the depths of his heart, he declared: 'Don't say he desired to practice the Way; say that he retired.' The counselor was overjoyed when he summoned me, and said: 'It was a wonder! I've never seen such concern on the part of his lordship! You should be grateful. Choose your successor quickly.' Upon hearing this, I went and had the present Kudayū [Shōsan's successor] greet him immediately. You have to be decisive or you won't get results.

"Although I, too, started off shaving my head in this way, having come this far, I now think that practicing while in public service is better after all. On the other hand, I don't worry about what I should do or what people think.

"As I said, I became a monk and made pilgrimages around the country, sleeping in fields and mountains and paying little attention to my appearance. For a while I became a monk of the Precepts (Risshū) sect and abused myself physically. When I was engaged in Ritsu discipline on Chidori Mountain in the province of Mikawa, I lived on nothing but barley gruel and boiled barley with rice. Because of the way I lived, my body was exposed to wind and rain, my stomach and intestines were affected by the raw food, and I became ill. My illness finally grew severe. Though I tried many different remedies, I was unable to make a complete recovery. All of the many doctors I saw simply gave up. I, too, thought I would die. When I had reached what seemed the end of my rope, when it appeared there was no way to keep me alive, my relatives in the area gathered for a meeting. Since my younger brother was an eminent physician, he came when he was informed of my condition. I didn't need medicine or anything else, he said, but would improve with a nourishing diet. When I asked what he meant by a nourishing diet, he replied that he meant meat. I told him that I would eat a corpse if it meant a speedy recovery, and followed his instructions. It took two years for me to recuperate completely, which I managed without taking any medicine. What's more, after that I abstained from eating meat and have continued to do so ever since. I was severely criticized by people at that time. I was about to die, but nourishing myself like a 'shameless Shōsan,' I was able to remain alive to this day and practice diligently. Without a decisive mind, nothing is realized."

After this, the samurai visited the Master many times to hear his teaching and eventually came to agree with him. He gave up the idea of becoming a monk and concentrated on performing his duties, considering them as religious practice. *{pp. 238–242}*

Shōsan was karmically disposed to become a monk

One day a monk [from the assembly] asked: "You always say that a samurai is well suited to religious practice while a monk is not, and refuse to ordain anyone. People want to know why *you* took the tonsure. How should I respond to them?"

The Master listened and said: "One of you try to respond."

A monk replied: "I would say, because there is greater merit for a monk than for a lay person in awakening the Buddha Dharma."

The Master said: "That was not the reason. Shōsan shaved his head simply because of his karma. Presumably, Shōsan was karmically disposed to become a monk. I shaved my head because I wanted to do it more than anything. . . ." *{p. 244}*

Because of my cowardice, I have come this far

In an evening talk, the Master said: "At first I thought the zazen of emptying the mind was correct and practiced it for a long time. Then, one day, I realized that the Way of no-thought and no-mind could not surpass the Way of Shakyamuni Buddha himself. The Buddha did use various thoughts in his sermons throughout his life. Based on his understanding of right and wrong, he practiced the Way of no-thought. His was not a vacant state. Equipped with this new understanding, I applied the warrior's glare, and my cowardliness diminished somewhat.

"All of you should also distinguish right from wrong and practice the zazen of no-thought in all your activities. I used to be quite unhappy about the fact that I wasn't able to retire to the mountains, but now I feel it was lucky. If I'd retired in that way, I would have become a good practitioner, but remained ignorant of my faults. Having stayed within society, I have realized my insufficiencies and my deluded nature."

After a pause, he added: "Still, there's one thing I'm not satisfied with. From the beginning, my character has been such that I cannot forget about death. Wherever I am, I can never let down my guard. I surpass others only in my aversion to death. That's why I practice with the 'warrior's glare.' Actually, it is because of my cowardice that I have come this far." *{p. 249}*

A remarkable woman

In an evening talk, the Master said: "Isn't so-and-so's mother a remarkable woman? The other day she said that something has come over her. All of a sudden she will feel a certain rush of energy, and gets urges to do things like breaking the ceramic pot she uses for carrying water. Even her appearance has improved. Today she went into the next room and found the other women idly chatting. She said, 'What lazy people! You should make use of *this* energy.' And she stood there mimicking the *Niō*. I happened to notice it, and it didn't seem at all peculiar. You would think it a little strange to see a woman imitating the *Niō*, but it wasn't strange at all. I felt she had received some of the *Niō's* energy, or else she couldn't have acted like that. All of you should try to mimic the *Niō* as you stand there, and you will see what I mean. You'll look quite ridiculous!

"The other day, this woman told me about a statue of [one of] the *Niō* that she had had made. The statue had just arrived, and when she looked at it, she was instantly transformed by its energy. She said that she felt as if she had spit out everything. And, in fact, I saw that her expression had changed. Anyone who didn't know her would have sworn she was a madwoman." {p. 253}

Fusan receives the Master's energy

One day the Master said: "Buddhism means making use of everything. Samurai, in particular, should make use of 'zazen amid the cry of battle.'"[27] Having said this, the Master demonstrated it. His disciple Fusan,[28] who was present at the time, received the Master's energy with a firm resolve. Later, the Master heard about this and acknowledged Fusan's understanding." {p. 272}

All delusion arises when you relax your vital energy

In the spring of the second year of Keian (1649), some monks from the Sōtō sect asked about the essential practice of Dharma. The Master instructed them, saying: "In Buddhist practice we carefully guard the self. In the Sōtō sect, older monks and novices alike say, 'Let go of the self.' These are good words. Based on these words, I wrote in Kusawake [Parting of the Grasses], 'Don't forget the self.' Look carefully into this stage of practice. The importance of practice lies solely in guarding the self with care. All delusion arises when you relax your vital energy. So firmly fix your gaze and don't relax your vital energy throughout the day. Remain sharp and alert while guarding the self, and the six rebellious delusions will be annihilated. You should guard it so thoroughly that even in your dreams you don't let down your guard. Though you think your guard is sufficiently up, you may relax unknowingly and be overcome by delusion. Your horse-consciousness will run wild in a field of delusion; and your monkey-mind will prance about on branches of fame and fortune. Resolutely open your eyes, let the phrase 'Don't be deluded'[29] be your reins, brace yourself sternly, and keep up your guard. Don't relax your vital energy for even a moment!" {p. 139}

* * *

There is an apparent contradiction when Shōsan stresses not forgetting the self and guarding the self and at the same time praises the Sōtō Zen expression "Let go of the self." For Shōsan, however, guarding the self is an important preliminary step in the practice of letting go of the self. At least he expresses it as a preliminary step, though one has the feeling that he believes that both statements are equivalent. He tries to take Zen out of the realm of ideas in which statements like "Let go of the self" can become traps.

Monks, today especially, have deep-rooted preta-*minds*

Again addressing the Sōtō monks, the Master said: "I, too, know nothing of things like satori. And though you don't seek such things either, you have obtained birth as human beings and received the benefit of being allowed to become monks; so you should somehow save yourselves from the world of *pretas*.[30] Monks, today especially, have deep-rooted *preta*-minds. From the time they are novices, they crave acknowledgment of their excellence. This desire to surpass others is the *preta* that covets wisdom. Then there are the *pretas* that seek to lead the congregation, the *pretas* that seek to become high priests, the temple *pretas* (those attached to their temple), the Dharma-flag-waving *pretas*, and the recluse *pretas*. With these thoughts as their foundation, they create all kinds of *preta*-minds. Even when things are in order, these people are ill at ease. All their lives they are tormented by the pain these *pretas* cause. They are pulled around by these *preta*-thoughts throughout eternity. All these people will fall into the Three Evil Paths.[31] Under all circumstances, be careful to escape the way of the *pretas*. And do not let people arouse your worldly desires. They may say: 'I shall make you senior priest,' or 'You are quite advanced in your practice. It would be regrettable if you stopped studying the scriptures.' Or they may offer to show you how to prosper. These are all people whose worldly desires have been aroused. Nowadays there is not one person who will besiege worldly desires. They are all aroused by desire for name and fame. Take care not to be aroused by worldly desires!" {*pp. 139–140*}

Jōshū's Mu

One day the Master instructed a monk: "For monks, looking into a kōan is a good way to practice. You should study Jōshū's *Mu*,[32] applying your energy forcefully throughout the day. Whatever you're doing, hold onto

Mu Mu Mu Mu. Practice so hard that you don't even slacken when asleep. Above all, keep watch over death, and you won't go wrong." {p. 140}

Let the truth reveal itself

One day the Master said: "Beginners should let the truth reveal itself at all costs. Before the truth reveals itself, you should not engage in unreasonable practices or excessive zazen. If you try to force your vital energy to reveal itself and you become involved in austere practices, your resolve will break down and your vital energy will diminish. It will be useless, and that will be the end of it. All of you should keep this in mind. When you are feeling bad, your resolution will be weaker than usual.

"Religious practice is the nurturing of your vital energy. That's why an ancient master[33] said: 'Nurture it for a long time.' You should never let your vital energy diminish. There are innumerable people nowadays indulging in unreasonable practices, doing skeletal zazen, while their vital energy is reduced and they become invalids and madmen. Instead, just let your aspiring heart advance, and allow the truth to reveal itself." {p. 140}

Guard your robust spirit

One day the Master said: "Practice means making the greatest possible use of your robust spirit. The so-called six rebels steal the original Mind at the six sites.[34] These rebels appear in vulnerable places in your mind. That's why we should strengthen our vital energy and guard our minds vigorously. People all misunderstand this. When told of impermanence, they lose their courage. When told of nonthinking, they become superficial monks. This is a great mistake. Guard your robust spirit whenever possible." {p. 140}

Practice till body and mind are no more

A recluse came and asked: "What is the primary concern in religious practice?" The Master responded: "Put everything aside and only study death. Always study death, free yourself from death, and when death really comes you will not be flustered. In order to save others, knowledge is necessary. For your own salvation, however, whatever knowledge you have grasped becomes your enemy. Just be [mindless] as earth; recite the *nenbutsu* [praise to Amida Buddha] and study death."

The recluse said: "I'm always reading *Mōanjō* [A Safe Staff for the Blind]. Is it wrong to read this?"

The Master then said: "Whatever you read and commit to memory will be an obstacle. You should just recite the *nenbutsu* and make dying easy." The recluse said: "I no longer have evil thoughts or desires."

The Master responded: "You put things in order to a small extent and think it's a good thing. However much your desires disappear and you become a good man, you won't rid yourself of thoughts of worldly enjoyment or self. If you can't separate yourself from these thoughts, they will produce the karma leading you to transmigration. To destroy these thoughts, keep watch as though they were sworn enemies; constantly attack them with the *nenbutsu*. You need no other theories. You need no knowledge. You're not going to attain Buddhahood through anyone's favor, nor is anyone going to drag you down to hell. Your own present thoughts will carry you to heaven or to hell. Wrath is the hell-dweller, greedy mind is the *preta*, grumbling is the beast: These are called the three evil paths. Taken together with the three righteous paths—*asura* [fighting demons], humans, and heavenly beings—they constitute what we call the six realms. These six realms are all within one mind. Not leaving this sphere, ascending and descending, going around nonstop, is called transmigrating through the six realms. You should know this by the fact that right now your own mind is transmigrating. A virtuous thought quickly becomes an evil thought, and an evil mind becomes a virtuous mind. This is proof that you descend from heaven to hell and ascend from hell to heaven. In similar fashion, you transmigrate through other realms. To be detached from this mind, becoming unborn and undying, is called Buddhahood. This is the way one studies the roots of thoughts till they are exhausted and attains Buddhahood. How can anyone else stop your thoughts? You should firmly fix your gaze, recite *Namu Amida Butsu Namu Amida Butsu*,[35] drive yourself as though your life depended upon it, and cut off the roots of your thoughts. Acts of extreme evil and desires for what is unattainable will cease. But there will still be something remaining. It is a difficult thing to cut off the roots of your thoughts. So make this bag of excrement [the physical body] your enemy and destroy it with the *nenbutsu.*"

The recluse said: "Then we should understand that this body will be discarded."

The Master admonished him, saying: "To understand is wrong. The Buddha Way is not the understanding of anything, but rather the practice till body and mind are no more." {*pp. 141–142*}

Sutra recitation

One day, while reciting a sutra,[36] the Master said: "You should hold your body straight, let your vital energy settle at your navel, and fix your gaze. If you recite in this manner, you will be practicing meditation through your recitation. If you become an empty shell when you recite, you won't even gain merit." {*p. 142*}

There is no benefit in aimless wandering

One day a recently ordained monk took leave of the Master, saying he intended to become an unaffiliated monk, traveling around the country and begging for his food. The Master reprimanded him: "These thoughts that you have confided to me are outrageous and irrational. It's important for one who wants to practice the Way of the old Buddhas to seek a good teacher and mingle with good friends. But you have just recently decided to practice the Way, and without plan or means are going to wander aimlessly around the country. That I can't sanction. In olden times when students went on pilgrimages, they questioned teachers and sought out the Way, never considering their lives, traveling as much as thirty thousand miles. Others, having received the teachings, made pilgrimages around the country in order to deepen their understanding. Yet others, with strong foundations, made pilgrimages to test themselves further whenever a situation presented itself. Still others aspired to journey among mountains, rivers, grasses, and trees to cultivate their minds. But I've never heard of any benefit coming from wandering with no plan or means in the manner you propose. You will wander aimlessly here and there, walking around in confusion and ending as a scoundrel. When you can't avoid it, you will steal and soon become a criminal. Countless monks wandering around in this manner have become heretics or gone mad. I'm fed up with people like that. Even hearing about them disgusts me. If you understand my objections, you'll stay on. If you don't, there's no point in returning here. We'll have no connection now or in the next life."

Receiving such a strong admonition [from the Master], the petitioner finally decided to stay on at the temple. *(p. 142)*

Work-parties eliminate bad karma

One day, seeing the tired monks shouting "Heave-ho!" in unison during a temple work-party, the Master said: "Well, monks! Is it easier than chanting? Be clear about this. When chanting sutras, don't think even for a moment that it's bothersome. Lay people perform these labors daily in the course of their lives. It's wrong for monks to chant sutras and perform other practices in a routine manner." That evening, he added: "Work parties are good for eliminating the harmful effects of bad karma. If you don't destroy this bad karma, you won't progress in your religious practice." *(p. 145)*

The desire to practice the Way is a real treasure

During an evening talk, someone remarked: "Today's monks don't aspire to the [Buddha] Way."

Hearing this, the Master said: "Put the Way aside for the moment. There isn't even anyone who has really left home.[37] I say this because if they were asked to leave their temples, they'd all lose their presence of mind."

The previous questioner said: "Today's monks rebuke others if they receive insufficient contributions when performing funerals and memorial services."

The Master said: "Since they use these contributions to keep the [temple] functioning daily, there is some sense to this greed. But with regard to temples, the more they have, the more they suffer. The monks in charge of these temples begin to like [what they acquire]; they want

[more] and don't want to part with what they've got. They envy those who have things they lack. But desire to practice the Way is [the real] treasure. If you arouse this even to a small degree, worldly pleasures will become distasteful; you will no longer desire them, and you will even discard the temple. Even with that kind of attitude, one is not necessarily worthy to be called a practitioner; yet even people of this caliber aren't to be found. It goes without saying that no one trains himself to practice like a man-eating dog tearing unrelentingly [at its prey]." *(p. 147)*

Pay no heed to rising thoughts

One day the Master said: "All of you should focus on your present activity and practice vigorously. First, when you recite the *nenbutsu* you should say *Namu Amida Butsu Namu Amida Butsu* with all your energy. If you do this, before you realize it, your deluded thoughts will naturally cease. For example, a guest may drop in at a place where business is actively being conducted, but he will quickly return home. Even though deluded thoughts may naturally arise, if you practice vigorously and pay no attention to them, they will soon disappear. So pay no heed to rising thoughts. Focus on your present activity and practice. As the fruits of this effort grow, you will acquire the energy of zazen and will also understand the energy of the *Niō*." *(p. 149)*

Living in the mountains

One day the Master said to the assembly: "Years ago, I loved living in the mountains. If I saw even a small forest, I wanted to build a retreat there, and I did live in the mountains on occasion. But it wasn't written in the stars, and so I didn't end up there. Yet things have worked out fine. Had I lived in that manner, I would have become a good Buddhist while never understanding my faults. The fact that I had thought previously that living in the mountains was a good thing and now feel it not to be good is, I believe, a result of advancing in my practice.

A desire to retire to the mountains is symptomatic of a pretentious mind, a mind that seeks the exotic. It's the same as a layman making an elegant garden or elaborately decorating a parlor."

At that point someone said: "There's a monk at such and such a place now who, though quite eccentric, seems to speak clearly of true principles."

The Master responded: "If you practice speaking, you can speak about anything. Buddhists today think that clever arguments are fine, and others respect them for being adept at this. Actually there isn't anything more useless than clever arguments. In fact, they become a great source of resentment. When I was young, I, too, made a great mistake here, and I often fell into clever argumentation." {p. 150}

With the nenbutsu *alone, you can exhaust the self completely*

To a monk, Jihon, from the province of Nō[38] who was about to leave the Master's temple, he said: "These are my final words to you: Never teach of salvation in a future world of which you are not [yet] a part. Just rouse the truth within yourself and show it to others. As a rule, you will have trouble even in this life when you pretend to be what you are not. Just recite the *nenbutsu* so completely that you are released from your self. By being released from your self, I mean that while reciting *Namu Amida Butsu Namu Amida Butsu*, you study death. Death opens up and is clarified. You, too, are treasuring your fundamental self. It doesn't require a lot of time. With the *nenbutsu* alone, you can exhaust this self completely." {p. 151}

*   *   *

Shōsan here is playing on the monk's name, which means "fundamental self." An alternative reading for the final sentences could be: "You, too, are treasuring Jihon. . . . With the nenbutsu *alone, you can exhaust Jihon completely."*

Discriminating thinking

In an evening talk during the summer of the year of the rabbit (1651), the Master said: "At some time, I'm not sure when, my discriminating thinking just stopped. I no longer speak from analytical knowledge. So although I do err in what I say at times, I've come this far, meeting things as they arise, and haven't been without success. From my youth, I have generally been of a nondiscriminating character. Still, when heartfelt communication takes place, with one phrase, I have often had the final say over those who are always using analytical knowledge. I myself find it very strange. But saying things that cut through to the core is something I've always been strong at. When a subject is being discussed, I listen, quickly grasp the essence, and make a statement that cuts right through it." {p. 151}

My energy has tempered a bit

One day the Master said: "Until around the spring of last year, my vital energy was like the pull of a strong bow, or like the charge of a good quality horse. Stretched firmly, this energy was ready to spring forth. This year, that vital energy seems to have tempered a bit, but I don't see signs that it has slackened. I think it has actually ripened somewhat." {p. 151}

See it all as nothing special

One day a monk said: "Lately when I travel on pilgrimage, I long for the friends I have left behind."

The Master listened, and responded: "If a temporary separation feels like this, how much more pain will you feel when you die and proceed alone on your journey through the underworld, not knowing what lies ahead? Surely that will be painful. You should consider all this beforehand."

He added: "Since your mind changes like that, you have to cultivate it to some degree. Observe it diligently, practice hard, and don't concern yourself about anything, whatever it is. See it all as nothing special. In any event, you must arouse the great matter. Arouse it, and this great matter allows you to make use of everything." {pp. 151–152}

Observing life and death is itself the cutting edge

One day the Master said to a visitor: "There are many among my critics who are skillful in speech and clever at theorizing. But not one of them engages in religious practice. Previously, at my retreat at Ishinotaira, when I tried to teach a bit of theory, everyone became a Buddhist theorist, so I gave it up. I stopped teaching Buddhist theory and from then on recommended practice only. As a result, I dislike cleverness in Buddhism. I consider only those who have the energy for sudden awakening to be vessels of the Dharma.

"To rid yourself of clinging is especially essential to the Way of Zen. This means always being ready to act. Observing life and death is itself the cutting edge. And Zen energy, too, is this cutting edge." {p. 152}

Detach yourselves from your minds and bodies

One day two young samurai attendants came and asked about the essential points of the Dharma. The Master said: "Religious practice is detachment from this body. From the start, young people should not prize the body. It would be good to apprentice yourselves to lords. If you become used to sacrificing yourselves for little things, gaining as much merit as possible, you will be able to sacrifice yourselves freely anywhere you go. If you just detach yourselves from your minds and bodies, you will attain Buddhahood." {p. 152}

Just throw it away

One day someone came and said that he had repeatedly requested to be put in a bag and cremated when he died. The Master, hearing this, remarked: "In ancient times there was a famous warrior from a foreign country. He made a request similar to yours and was buried in that manner. Somebody at that time composed a song that criticized him by saying that though he could die, he couldn't throw away his body. So just throw it away. You'd be better off requesting that your body be fed to dogs and birds."

The fellow then said: "I don't think that I would want to expose this ugly thing."

The Master responded: "If that is your inclination, there is all the more reason to expose it—so that people can see it. In the path of 'repentance through shame,' you expose your hateful side. If you know it's ugly, why not just throw it out in disgust? When all is said and done, corpses are pretty. There's nothing so repulsive as a living body. Eye fluid, nasal discharge, feces, and urine—not one of these is clean. Internally, the mind piles up only bad karma. Shouldn't you say, 'What a bag of excrement!' scowl at it, and throw it out in disgust?" *(p. 153)*

* * *

Most pronouncements of one's detachment subtly (and sometimes not so subtly) convey the opposite message. Shōsan is quick to bring this to the attention of the student by using the parable of the warrior.

The great matter

Once, at dawn, the Master said to the congregation: "Though it doesn't always happen, there are times when I'm pressed with the death-energy. At daybreak, the 'great matter' rising from below my navel and clogging my chest makes it difficult to breathe."

At that time a monk asked: "Is what you call the great matter, the great matter of life and death?"

The Master responded: "It's not what I *call* the great matter. It simply *is* the great matter." *(p. 154)*

Pretas *and beasts surround me*

One day someone came and said: "Having heard about you for some time, I have come all this way to make a humble request. Please honor me with one verse."

The Master replied: "If one person says something without any foundation in truth, ten thousand people take it to be fact. If a fool says Shōsan is a distinguished fellow and it is spread to the far corners of the country, people start thinking that Shōsan can fly through the air and emit light. Then they come to observe Shōsan and, seeing an ordinary old man, are disappointed. The fact is that I'm just an ordinary Zen monk. However, though I don't want to die, I want to practice so that when I'm faced with death, I'll think nothing of it—I'll stick out my neck and die freely. But, forgetting about death for the moment, I can't even escape the world of *pretas* and beasts. Are those who want to escape from these worlds superior to those who exist without even a thought of doing so?

I'm not superior to anybody. If you're inclined to listen to my advice, you should first become a complete beginner."

Thinking that the Master was hiding something, the questioner was even more eager to hear his teaching.

The Master said: "I don't know the value of the Buddha Way, but when it comes to my faults, I know them only too well. If you want to associate with me and come here as you please, you'll have to be prepared to hear over and over about my regret that *pretas* and beasts surround me. I know nothing else of any value. You may think I'm just being humble, but I'm actually sinking into the lowest pit of hell."

The Master then said: "You appear to be a person who observes the Buddha Dharma. Express yourself."

The questioner said he knew nothing.

The Master urged: "You're holding something back; let it out right away!"

The questioner said: "I received Jōshū's [kōan] 'Wash your begging bowl'[39] from a certain head priest and have thrown myself into it completely."

The Master responded: "A monk is one of the three treasures offered to the people of the world; but one who receives worthless [teachings] will inevitably cause others harm. It's not that you can't penetrate such phrases, but that even if you do, you won't be able to eliminate the *preta* and beast minds. I, too, have experienced some degree of penetration into my own nature. But it is of no use to me. Nowadays, those who have the experience of seeing into their own nature (*kenshō*) are generally harmful to others. You should just become as earth and practice reciting the *nenbutsu*."

The questioner asked: "What is religious practice?

The Master responded: "Exhaust the I."

The questioner asked: "What does it mean to become as earth?"

The Master responded: "Throwing out all your knowledge and your delusions and with *Namu Amida Butsu Namu Amida Butsu*, erasing reason, erasing the I and becoming one with the empty sky—that is being as earth and is the religious practice of Buddhahood."

The Master then said: "Nowadays, there are many people here and there who teach the Buddha Dharma casually. As for myself, I have nothing to teach. The value of coming to my place is to learn that there is nothing whatever to become. That's what I teach. But I don't leave things unattended. Since it is the one great matter, I'm determined not to lose the seed even through many lives. I hold firmly to the aspiration to ultimately attain the wisdom of Buddhahood. You, too, should just become a chanter of the *nenbutsu*. Hōnen said he knew of no other way to Buddha wisdom than the *nenbutsu*, and he even wrote this in his *Ichimai kishō, Nimai kishō*, and *Sanmai kishō*.[40]

I, too, think highly of the *nenbutsu*. With this practice, you'll no longer be afflicted with disease. You should exert energy reciting *Namu Amida Butsu Namu Amida Butsu*, as though a large bell were ringing in your chest. And no expression of evil thoughts should appear on your face. If you practice this regularly, your thoughts will be destroyed. Though it is wrong to use Chinese characters to explain the *nenbutsu*, it seems new to you, so I will discuss it. As the two characters *nen* and *butsu* are written, they mean 'to think of the Buddha.' People don't usually think of the Buddha. Everyone thinks of this present world. Minds that are occupied with this present world are planting seeds that spawn the evil paths. You should realize that your mind is transmigrating in the evil paths right now. There are times when you feel energetic, times when you feel weak, times when you are angry, times when you are greedy, and times when you are envious of others. If you enjoy the evil paths in this way and travel through them, you won't remain in the human realm. Even if you obtain the benefits of heaven, for example, you'll soon fall into hell. This is because good thoughts may occur for a while, but they soon become evil. If you fail to cut off these thoughts at their roots, there will be no way to escape transmigrating. You should recite the *nenbutsu* as much as you can and exhaust all thoughts. Even if just a few thoughts remain, you'll find yourself reborn in a world created by those thoughts."

The Master then said: "You have a vulnerable nature. If you are praised by others, your nose becomes long [you become proud] and you run around sprouting horns [you become demonic]. There isn't anyplace you go where you aren't praised. No one ever criticizes you severely the way I do. The value of having met me is that you've learned never to be adversely affected by others' praise. That's why I've spoken to you in this manner."

That evening the Master said to the congregation: "Wasn't that fellow this morning overly intellectual? It's difficult for someone with that type of nature to enter the Buddha Way. The more one talks to him, the more he rationalizes. In his case, without the rod, nothing will happen. If, when speaking to him, one hammers home each point, he'll improve a bit. Were I a regular teacher, I might have made more of an impression on him."

At that time a monk said: "I don't like to come into contact with people who have so many disorders."

The Master, hearing this, said: "For me, the more difficult the person, the better. I want to meet people who give Shōsan the third degree. Unfortunately I've yet to meet anyone who could stagger me." {pp. 154–156}

The Buddha Dharma applies to criminals, too

One day in the third month of the year of the dragon, a samurai retainer came and said: "My lord listened to your talks and was able to understand them quite well. However, the elder samurai of our clan, not having any understanding of the Way, kill people for trivial offenses."

The Master listened, and replied: "Is that so? Regardless of how much your lord is attracted to the Dharma, if he can't control those under him, and consequently they kill someone for a minor offense, his coming here is of no value. If that's the case, tell him he can't come here again. After all, one who listens to the Buddha Dharma understands that you don't just kill someone that lightly. No matter who the criminal is, if you really want to help him, you will put some obstacle in the way of the executioner—for the Buddha Dharma applies to that criminal, as well. If you want to save someone, there is always a way. But when someone gets pleasure from killing, he will say that he can't save the perpetrator of even a minor crime and will allow him to be killed. How immoral! One person killed is a grave matter." {p. 156}

I don't place any importance on ghosts and spirits

In an evening talk, the Master said: "There is no progress in religious practice. Forty years ago, when I was at Saijō Temple in Sekimoto in the province of Sō, there was a report of a great dragon in the sea at Oda-wara.[41] Hearing this, I confidently took a small boat with the intention of ripping out the beast's horns. I also planned to pass through the Mount Fuji Cave.[42] In my youth I acted fearlessly, but it served no useful purpose. Thinking back on it, I was very serious about all those adventures. Now I have no taste for them. They are nothing but trouble."

Again he said: "From the time I was young, I never placed any importance on ghosts and spirits." {p. 157}

Religious practice in pursuit of satori is dangerous

One day a monk came and asked: "I heard that a certain monk died while studying a kōan, thus becoming a spirit. Does that make sense?"

The Master responded: "If one dies seeking satori, that certainly can happen. In any case, religious practice in pursuit of satori is dangerous." {p. 158}

Recite the nenbutsu single-mindedly

In an evening talk, a monk said: "As I travel through town, there are many useless objects that I think I would like."

The Master responded: "That's because of habits that develop from long periods of dwelling in the world of *preta*."

Someone else then remarked: "I, too, work very diligently at destroying this feeling of greed, but no matter what I do, it won't go away."

The Master said: "You shouldn't go against those feelings. You should just recite the *nenbutsu* single-mindedly. If you accumulate merit from the *nenbutsu*, you will rid yourself of everything." {p. 158}

The coward's Dharma

In an evening talk, the Master said to the congregation: "Do you know what it is that operates in universal virtue? Can you tell me the substance of it?"

A lay disciple answered: "Virtue is liberation."

The Master said: "Put liberation aside for the moment. You would have been better off saying that it is no-mind and no-thought. Everything is derived from this. When there is no-mind and no-thought, everything is in harmony. When I hear clapping to a beat, for example, I become a part of it. And when I sing, 'Here is the wandering monk walking through all the provinces,'[43] I become one with that feeling. Though I do not know how to hold a fan [in the appropriate way for the dance], with a heart that dances freely, I can throw myself into the dance, becoming one with the tune. Allowing the form to manifest in accord with the situation also applies in the realm of no-thought. For example, someone who loves to dance comes along and says: 'I love to dance and would like to be shown how to attain Buddhahood through dancing.' If I didn't show him, I would not be acting in accord with universal virtue."

In connection with this, the Master said: "I've had the experience of being asked by someone who liked to hunt how he could attain Buddhahood through hunting. I said: 'Is it fun when the birds fly around in a frenzy crying *kyaa kyaa* every time you kill one of them? If so, will you enjoy yourself when you also are about to die? If you're happy when you die, that's Buddhahood. Buddhahood is dying with a calm mind. Therefore every time you kill a beast of prey, you should feel as though your own bones are being crushed and you are preparing to die with it, laughing in the face of death. That's the attitude of a true hunter.' When I said that it was a strange warrior who didn't hunt in this manner, he was in a quandary. He stopped hunting and later progressed in his religious practice.

"I didn't learn this universal virtue from anyone. But I suffered because I wasn't prepared to die. So I trained myself in various practices and came to understand the principle. My way is the coward's Dharma."
{pp. 160–161}

Use the Niō *mind to arrest the six rebellious delusions*

One day the Master said: "Though ordinary people originally possess the unperturbed *Tathagata* mind, they are attacked and stripped of this mind by the six rebellious delusions. Therefore, if you use the mind of the *Niō* to arrest the six rebellious delusions, your original mind will develop naturally. For example, [in a castle] when a guard armed with a staff stands by the entrance, chamber guards occupy the inner hall, and other guards situate themselves at different places to protect the lord, the lord can live in peace. *Niō* zazen is the meditation of the *Tathagata*'s foot soldiers. First learn this foot-soldier zazen.

"In the parlor, there are also the sixteen virtuous gods,[44] the four heavenly kings[45] and the protector gods of the various levels of original mind. And there are twelve divine generals who bear the 'twelve branches' on their heads and stand guard during the twelve periods.[46] When they stand guard throughout the twenty-four hours of the day, delusions are abolished and the central Buddha image is secure. Without acquiring this *Niō* energy, you cannot defeat delusion. I'm determined to present this teaching of the Buddha images to the authorities. I want to do it even if I have to become a ghost in order to make my point." {p. 161}

Satori isn't everything

One day the Master said: "People today think that if they don't attain satori, Buddhism has no value. They are mistaken. Buddhism means making good use of your mind right now; it means activating the mind to function in the present. Indeed, making steadfast use of your mind vigorously is what I call religious practice. The stronger your mind, the more accessible it becomes. Hard practice brings great merit. Meager practice brings small merit. For example, though some may receive a stipend of ten thousand *koku* [of rice], if you receive a thousand *koku*, it is still better than a hundred. You receive your fair share of the merit. Some people think that if you have a satori experience, you enter the domain of the Buddha. However, they are mistaken. Though you may have the understanding, you may not have the freedom to use it. The domain of the Buddha is something exceptional. But even if you don't seek satori, you should practice and receive merit." {p. 162}

Face to face with death

One day the Master said: "Religious practice is nothing other than the capacity [to arouse] fearless energy. Without this energy, whatever practices you perform, whatever virtuous feelings you have, all are without substance. There can't be much difference between *Tathagata* Zen and *Niō* Zen. One expresses itself in your mind [*Tathagata* Zen], and the other in your face [*Niō* Zen]. Without this energy, will you be prepared when you come face to face with death in your ordinary state of mind? How then will you persevere over other hardships? Having cultivated this vital energy quickly, I thought I could transfer it to others quickly, too. But none of you has obtained it. It seems to be as difficult to transfer it to others as it is to practice it oneself."

At that time, someone asked: "What can we do to cultivate this vital energy?"

The Master replied: "You cannot do anything other than fix your gaze and study death. Make this bag of excrement your enemy and keep it constantly under siege. Note carefully where I wrote 'Throw out the body' and 'Guard the self,'[47] and practice it. This energy will naturally manifest itself." *{pp. 163–164}*

A *living corpse*

In an evening talk, someone remarked: "I have never worried about death."

Hearing this, the Master said: "Though that may seem good to you, you will make no progress in your practice. Because of my own dread of death, I wanted to be a living corpse. That's how I was able to involve myself in religious practice. As long as I have a body that is subject to death, I will certainly have the vital energy to apply myself to practice through many lives. Though you say death doesn't disturb you, you are no Man of the Way. Though you think this is the Way, you don't know the master of the self—that which lets you freely use the six roots." *{p. 164}*

A *fixed reality*

In an evening talk the Master said: "Fixed reality[48] is difficult to disregard. When people, myself included, see houses, money, and everything else glittering before us, we can't think of them as nonexistent, however hard we try. Whatever the situation, if we fail to see our own true nature, we won't wake up from this idea of a fixed reality. Though there have been times when I've experienced this truth, I'm unable to make free use of it. With my fearless vital energy, I regularly fix my gaze on this bag of worms [my body] when walking, standing, sitting, or lying down.[49] Even when urinating and defecating, I'm never neglectful. I realize what an idiotic bag of pain the body is, but I'm not free of it yet. Though my understanding is slight, it's still enough to work with." {p. 166}

Prepare yourself for death at any moment

One day when the Master arrived at a certain place, there was a report that, while en route to one of his fiefs, the chief magistrate of the local clan had died following a mild illness. The Master listened in amazement and said: "Oh, the countless miseries! Believing that we and the world truly exist, it's hard to foresee the pain of sudden death. How tragic! This makes me feel that even with a slight aspiration for the Way, if you prepare yourself to die at any moment, you will still derive a great deal of merit."

That day there was a lot of feasting, and that evening the Master said: "All day, people have been recklessly eating and drinking. Their stomachs will be torn apart by Yama, king of the world of the dead." {p. 166}

One who thinks nothing of death is still steeped in karma

One day a monk asked: "In the case of an ordinary person, is it better for him to lament over his impending death or not to give it a second thought?"

The Master said: "One cannot be sure in every case, but in general, someone who expresses sorrow when he is about to meet death will be exhausting his karma and hence will gradually improve himself. But one who thinks nothing of death is still steeped in karma. Even a criminal confronting the possibility of the death penalty thinks nothing of it [when he commits his crime]." {pp. 166–167}

Live having let go of your life

In an evening talk, the Master said: "Perhaps it's because I have applied it since my youth that I can make free use of the Way of valor. It's easy to throw away your life in the heat of battle when you are facing an adversary, but not so easy to throw yourself off a cliff and die for nothing. This makes me think how difficult it is to throw away your body in the practice of Buddhism. That's why it is written in the Sutra of Forty-Two Chapters[50] that it is difficult to give up your life at the moment of death. In fact, very few die willing to let go their hold on life. Almost all people die unwilling to part with life. How very important this is! You monks should live having let go of your lives." {p. 167}

Farming is itself Buddhist activity

One day in the eighth month of the first year of Jōō (1652), the Master went to the Hōshōzen Temple in Hatodani in the province of Musashi.[51] At that time, many farmers from the area gathered to ask about the essentials of the Dharma.

The Master said: "Farming is itself a Buddhist activity. There is no need to seek practice elsewhere. Your body is the Buddha body, your mind the Buddha mind, and your work the Buddha-Work. Yet a single negative feeling can cause you to fall into hell in spite of the many good deeds you accomplish. Isn't it regrettable how emotions like hate, love, regret, and desire produce negative feelings that make you suffer day and night in this present life and cause you to fall into hell for all eternity? That's why you should awaken the great vow to destroy karmic hindrances through farming. If you cultivate the land, reciting *Namu Amida Butsu* with every movement of the hoe, you will surely reach Buddhahood. Just leave everything to Providence, be honest, and do not arouse personal desires. If you follow this advice, you will receive the blessings of heaven and enjoy a good life now and in the next world. These days, people tend to say that you cannot get through life on honesty alone. That's absolutely false. I haven't heard of anyone since antiquity who starved to death while maintaining a path of integrity. In the past as well as the present, those who have been dishonest have ruined their families and themselves. And poverty need not be scorned. I've never heard of anyone who died of starvation just because he was poor. The richer the household, the greater the misfortune, and the larger the number of tragic deaths. Besides, poverty and prosperity are karmically determined. Why would anyone foolishly arouse evil passions? At any rate, you should resolve that there is nothing more painful than starving to death as a result of wrongdoing; then, let go of everything, maintain your integrity at all costs, and cultivate your fields. Though everyone fears starvation, there is nothing more peaceful. Your desire for food lasts two or three days. After that, your consciousness fades and it's like falling asleep. You die at ease and without pain. Do you think dying is generally that easy? It's painful to die of a tumor. It's painful to die of diarrhea. It's painful to die of an insect bite. And it's painful to die of fever. None of these ways of dying is easy. Wouldn't it be easier to die of starvation than to endure one of these painful deaths?"

That evening, the Master turned to the people around him and said: "I wonder how strong were the aspirations of those who founded this temple. No one lacking deep inspiration or any thought of pursuing the Way could have done it. I want to urge Buddhism on anyone who even slightly aspires to the Way—even if it's coercion. I want to have it enter his bosom; I want to make it live." {pp. 168–169}

Don't lose yourselves to this world

One day the Master said: "People everywhere forget about death. They think that being alive today, they'll be alive tomorrow, too. Everyone is sure that death will not confront him in the present. How absurd! Thinking in this manner, such people don't maintain a grip on death; nor are they prepared when their time comes. They're like you. You think this ephemeral body is your own, this temporary world is your world, and you can play around in it forever. You go on like this, and suddenly, without warning, hell's messenger arrives. He attacks your internal organs, tearing them apart, and in the end, takes your life. When this happens, you'll grow dizzy, your hearing will become weak, your tongue will contract, and your whole body will be racked with the pain of approaching death. Not only will you suffer unbearable physical agony and begrudge your life, sorry to leave this world, but in front of you and behind you will be utter darkness with nowhere to go. Having lost your composure, you won't be able to bear the hardships you'll confront on your journey through the underworld. You'll give up thoughts of the Pure Land and fall like a beast into darker and darker places. Won't it be horrible to be plagued with the body of a *preta* or a beast? Surely you should dread that! But through extreme negligence you'll ignore this important matter and lose yourself in this foolish world, unaware of the implications of your acts. Consider this carefully. Take charge of this important matter, and be aware. Don't forget it and lose yourself to this world!" {pp. 169–170}

Make the one character death the master in your heart

In an evening talk, the Master said: "The Zen master Daie declared that we should keep the two characters for life and death in front of our noses and never forget them. The Zen master Hakusan instructed us to paste the character *death* on our foreheads.[52] Neither of these statements reflects powerful teaching. 'Keep the two characters in front of your nose' and 'Paste the character to your forehead' are substitutes for the real thing. It seems to me that Daie and Hakusan did not take to heart this great matter of life and death and practice vigorously. These expressions are weak. If I were to explain it, I'd say: 'Make the one character *death* the master in your heart, observing it and letting go of everything else.'"

A moment later, he said: "That still doesn't deal with it properly. Keeping it underfoot and constantly trampling it is the way to keep watch over this [great matter of life and death]. The image of *Bishamonten*[53] trampling on *Amanojaku*[54] is testimony to [the fact that one must keep death underfoot and trample it]." {p. 170}

When beginners easily experience satori

One day the Master said to the assembly: "It is a big mistake when beginners easily experience satori—when we allow the light to break through for them in a short time. Nowadays there are many [teachers] who do this. It's a frightening fact. I prefer simply to have students recite the *nenbutsu*, as in the Pure Land sects. That's why I start beginners with this recitation." {p. 170}

A woman's mind and the Buddha's mind are one

One day the Master said to a certain lady: "A woman's mind and the Buddha's mind are one. The ordinary mind, as it is, is the originally enlightened mind. The only difference lies in the way it is used. That's why you should make your mind ready by practicing *Niō* zazen.

Someone asked: "Is *Tathagata* zazen actually bad?"

The Master responded: "It's not bad. But if you teach a beginner advanced skills, it won't be effective for him. It's better for a beginner to start with *Niō* zazen." {p. 171}

Is it better to practice as a monk or a lay person?

One day someone asked: "Everything being equal, is it better to practice as a monk or a lay person?"

The Master responded: "Generally speaking, monks are two-fisted fighters, and lay people are one-fisted fighters. Lay people have more obstacles to practicing the Way than monks do. However, monks these days dislike Buddhism, and half the lay people lack interest in practicing the Way. What's more, most people's energy is slack, and their minds are tainted. But the samurai, serving his Master, has to maintain a strong, centered energy. In addition, he naturally keeps watch over death. In short, nowadays, religious practice is for lay people. Nonetheless, for one who seeks the truth, [being] a monk has an advantage." {p. 172}

Fix your gaze on Bodhidharma

During an evening talk, a monk asked: "When practicing zazen, is it all right not to work on a kōan or recite the *nenbutsu*, but instead apply the vital energy earnestly?"

The Master replied: "Of course. And if you act earnestly from this vital energy, kōans, *dharani*,[55] and *nenbutsu* will all be the same. You need only apply yourself to keeping this energy from sinking. If you want to keep this energy alive, fix your gaze on Bodhidharma[56] and do 'glaring' zazen." {p. 179}

The demon of birth and death

One day the Master said: "Practitioners today are always controlled by demons. You should guard yourselves constantly, warding off the demon of birth and death. An ancient master remarked: 'If the Bodhisattva doubts, an opportunity opens for the demon of birth and death.'"

A monk then asked: "What is the demon of birth and death?"

The Master responded: "That which creates the mind is the demon of birth and death." {p. 180}

Inscribing a wooden grave stupa

While the Master was inscribing a wooden grave stupa,[57] he remarked: "How absurd! Though it's going to happen to all of us, somehow we never believe that we, too, will die." {p. 181}

I alone am bad

During an evening talk, someone remarked: "Lord So-and-so's greed is unbecoming to a feudal lord."

The Master, hearing this, said: "You are walking around proclaiming your own shamefulness. When you call someone greedy, you are almost always taking part in the greediness yourself. I have never thought of anyone else as greedy. In this whole world, I think that I alone am greedy."

The fellow spoke again: "Lord So-and-so is a dunce and not fit to be governor of a large domain."

The Master said: "You really cannot see your error. If you were to administer that large domain yourself, you wouldn't do even one hundredth as well as he. It's silly for us, people of mere one- or two-hundred-*koku* stipends who clearly couldn't govern large domains, to be pointing the finger at others. It only reflects our lack of self-knowledge. I believe that I have never amounted to anything. That's why I've never thought that others are bad. I always think that I alone am bad." {p. 181}

Buddha Dharma fever

One day a certain man brought along someone who had "Buddha Dharma fever."[58] Referring to his companion, he said: "This fellow is an exceptional man of the truth. Please instruct him."

The Master said: "Oh, how disagreeable this 'truth' is! I'm sick and tired of the 'truth' of people around here. I'd rather welcome a rowdy fellow who's capable of slaughtering horses and cows." {p. 181}

A tale of a man who amused himself to death

One day there arrived a man who liked to jest. Noticing that one of the monks was ill, he said: "He's become ill because of his heretical behavior. There is an ancient tale in which a father, wondering how his children would react to his passing, pretended to die. His two sons mourned him and placed him in a coffin. One of them picked up the front of the coffin, the other lifted the back, and they started off. The father, no longer able to contain himself, began to laugh. The sons imagined that an evil spirit had entered the coffin, and without thinking, threw it down. At that moment, they happened to be passing the edge of a cliff, and the coffin fell into a valley, actually killing the father. This monk, too, is suffering from a disease that has resulted from a feigned illness."

The Master, hearing this, said: "That ancient tale is recited for people like *you*. That man died amusing himself doing something stupid. It's better to take things seriously, even though they may seem trivial. You, too, should become serious from now on." {pp. 182–183}

Dancing zazen

One day Elder Tetsu[59] asked: "When I am quietly sitting in zazen and my thoughts are not scattered, my energy sinks and I become sleepy. What can I do about this?"

The Master said: "Urge yourself to get up and do dancing zazen." {p. 183}

First encounter with death

One day, seeing a monk loafing, Shōsan scolded him, saying: "What's the use of allowing your vital energy to wane? From the time I began to crawl, I never let this energy wane. When I was four years old, my cousin, who was also four, died. At that time, I kept wondering where my dead cousin had gone and what had become of him." {p. 183}

Consideration of others

Someone arrived and told of a fellow who went to a poor monk to borrow a large sum of money. The Master, hearing this, said: "People are generally thoughtless creatures. If they themselves are poor, it should be natural for them to show consideration for others in the same circumstances. But in fact they do not. If it's someone else's money, they seem to think it can be gotten from rocks." {p. 183}

You will die!

One day a few old women came and asked about the essentials of Buddhism. The Master said: "I don't know anything I can teach you."

A moment later, he added unexpectedly: "You will die! You will die! Recite the *nenbutsu*. Never forget about death." {p. 185}

Throw away attachments

The Master was always chanting the *nenbutsu*. One day, an elder said: "Last night I had a dream in which there was a warning that the Master's chanting of the *nenbutsu* was useless."

The Master said: "I can see that you must feel my reciting the *nenbutsu* is wrong, if it even comes up in your dreams. This is because you have the wrong idea about it. When I say *Namu Amida Butsu Namu Amida Butsu*, I am saying: 'Throw away attachments, throw away attachments.' Is there anything wrong with that? I say *Namu Amida Butsu* rather than 'Throw away attachments' merely because it's not hard on the ears—and you react so strangely." {p. 185}

I, too, live off society

In the first month of the second year of Jōō (1653), the Master stopped at a Zen temple. At that time, some traveling entertainers arrived. The head priest told them: "Several people will soon be coming. You have to leave."

The entertainers pleaded: "Let us help celebrate!" But the head priest wouldn't allow it.

The Master then remarked: "Let them perform. That's the way they earn their living. In this world, we survive by helping each other. I, too, live off society, so it would be wrong for me to tell others they can't. Even though it's difficult to provide for one person with the little we have, if all of us come together, we can easily provide for each other. I, too, will give a ten-*sen* note."

The head priest was moved by the Master's words and allowed the entertainers to stay. {p. 234}

A mind absorbed in the folly of this world

One day the Master said: "There's no way to generate the vitality necessary for practice in one whose mind is absorbed in the folly of this world."

Then he clapped his hands, fixed his gaze, and said: "Oh, it's exhausting, it's exhausting! When you die, there's no way out of it. Everyone forgets this." {p. 235}

I know nothing about Buddhism

On the eighteenth day of the fifth month of the second year of Jōō (1653), a warrior from a certain district arrived and asked, "Why is it that Japanese Buddhism has become divided and no longer has a unifying thread?"

The Master responded: "Because nobody knows how to apply the Buddhist teachings, various Dharmas arise. If any of you who exert yourselves day and night were asked why you practice, could you answer in a few words? Well, how would *you* reply?"

The warrior started to think about it.

The Master, holding him in check, said: "If you say something now, it's too late. Because you don't have the thread in your mind, you cannot reply. If I were asked, I would say that being a coward, I practice simply because I do not want to die."

He continued: "That's all I ever say. I did write, in my *Tokuyū* (Meritorious Way of Life) and *Kusawake* (Parting of the Grasses), about attaining the unborn-undying mind.[60] However, because you do not guard your vital energy constantly, you have nothing to respond with. While all of you may listen to my teaching, you are reading and studying records of other Buddhist monks, comparing and measuring this and that and investigating other teachings. Not one of you comprehends my Dharma. You are all attracted to Buddhism. I know nothing about Buddhism. I only practice going beyond death."

After a pause, Shōsan said: "I am told that not one practitioner from your area comprehends my teaching; they all misunderstand me. When they come here before me, they appear as though they understand me. But they read records and discourses and practice various Buddhist teachings on their own, while none of them practices the Dharma according to my instructions. Moreover, they think that what I say is the same as what they read in those records and discourses. What I say is surely different. Just grit your teeth and investigate death thoroughly. From my youth until now—in my eightieth year—I have practiced nothing but this. My teaching is not [ordinary] Buddhism. If I were younger, I would travel to that area, find those people who have heard my talks, and say to them: 'Don't say you've heard Shōsan's talks—because you have misunderstood them. Don't talk about them under any condition.' I would tell them that Shōsan would object to the slightest mention of them." *(p. 238)*

The young grass-cutter and the short sword

At a funeral the Master said: "There is a tale of a young grass-cutter who ordered a short sword from a smith. Every time the boy returned from the mountains, he gave the smith a bundle of firewood. The smith, upon receiving the bundle, would give a blow to the sword with his hammer. In this way, after three years, the sword was completed. The boy cherished the sword, keeping it always by his side. One day, on his return from the mountains, the boy sat down to rest under a tall tree and went to sleep. There was a large serpent living in the tree who was on the verge of eating the boy. Suddenly, the sword released itself from its scabbard and lunged at the serpent's head. Startled, the serpent slithered away. A passerby saw this and waited for the boy to awaken. Desiring the boy's short sword, he traded his own long and short swords for it.

"This is certainly understandable. Though a mere short sword, it was a result of three years of quality workmanship and had become an excellent weapon. Anything whatsoever that is prepared with diligence has value. Religious practice, in particular, demands that you work exhaustively to accumulate merit. In this respect, I feel that even performing funeral services and prayers will have no effect if you haven't accumulated merit." {pp. 245–246}

Advice to a magistrate

One day Lord So-and-So came and said: "I am a magistrate, and my mind is always in turmoil. What can I do to attain peace of mind?"

The Master asked: "What keeps you so busy?"

The magistrate responded: "Figuring out policy together with my retainers and handing down judgments with them in accordance with policy."

The Master said: "If you try to figure things out that way, they will never get settled. Just use your mind resolutely, say whatever is on your mind, and always remain unobstructed. When a case is brought before you, brace yourself in preparation, empty your mind of everything, and listen to both sides. If you do that, like the reflection in a mirror, you will know in your heart how to resolve the case as soon as you hear it.

"In general, we are partial to ourselves and, as a result, can't judge anything correctly. If you would just decide cases straightforwardly, you wouldn't need any rest. At any rate, you shouldn't approach decisions hesitantly. If your decision is wrong, be prepared to cut open your belly. With your total attention, make decisions according to their merits. Guarding your everyday mind is, after all, extremely important." {p. 246}

Advice to a recluse who was fond of alcohol

One day the Master admonished a recluse who was fond of alcohol: "For many years I have been expressing my displeasure with your activities. Yet, shameful as they are, you will not give them up. How disgraceful! And now you stand in front of me with that expression on your face! This is surely your first birth as a human being. Well, I guess karma can't be altered. Still, there may be a way. Put a stone[61] or two of sake in a barrel.

Drink until you can drink no more. I will have other monks gather around you and chant sutras while they pour sake on your head until you feel tormented to the point of dying. Subjected to this degree of pressure, you may stop drinking. I will have them do it soon at Ushigome. As a rule, practitioners should refrain from smoking as well as drinking."

In this connection Shōsan added: "Formerly, when the priest Ban'an was in charge of Kiunji, he was a big drinker. When I expressed my displeasure and said he should give up alcohol, he replied: 'I agree that it's wrong, but people won't allow me to quit.'[62] I told him that even if it meant losing a parishioner, if he were faced with undue pressure, he should simply kick over the tray[63] and leave. Ban'an agreed, and when he found himself in such a situation, he remained firm and gave up drinking. In the end, the parishioners continued to entertain him, and not one of them left his parish.

"Practitioners should not enjoy activities that have no real purpose. Moreover, you should immediately cease any wrong actions that will be harmful to you." *{pp. 246–247}*

Eradication of the "I" is the true Dharma

One day a lay person asked: "I'm told that there are mistaken practitioners and true practitioners. How can we distinguish one from the other?"

The Master responded: "When the 'I' is eradicated, that is the true Dharma. Practitioners of wisdom establish a 'wise I.' Practitioners of compassion establish a 'compassionate I.' Practitioners of meditation establish a 'zazen I.' Practitioners of a [particular] viewpoint establish an 'I' with that viewpoint. Ordinary people tend to elevate themselves. One is always trying to *elevate* oneself above others. No matter how humble a person's position, if he upholds the truth, I will step aside for him." *{p. 247}*

The lady of the house becomes a true practitioner

During a conversation at someone's home, the Master said: "Nothing is more hopeless than the human condition. We can catch any one of numerous diseases, die from just about anything, and are subject to all kinds of karma. What a great misery it is!"

At that time the lady of the house was listening in amazement. Having been chronically sick, she wondered about her cause-and-effect relationship with the karmic body she had received. Thinking about the karma still lingering in her body, she became unsettled, and convinced herself that she must exhaust this karma. She invoked *dharani*, chanted sutras, beat and pinched herself until she was numb. With all her strength, she recited the *nenbutsu*, sutras, and *dharani* for some ten days, till one evening, confessing her sins before the Buddhist image in her personal shrine room, she was suddenly besieged by death pangs. Not allowing her energy to wane, she awoke to reality. Reminding herself that she must exhaust this karma, she stopped using servants and started doing things herself. She declared that she had been a wicked mistress, started working alongside her servants, and devoted herself to religious practice. Thereafter, her chronic illness disappeared and she was no longer feminine, but seemed like a man. The Master said that she had become a true practitioner." {p. 248}

Reciting sutras

One day during a sutra recitation, the Master instructed: "The true spirit of sutra reading occurs when you are in a settled state of mind. Forcefully reciting sutras in a loud voice or performing skeletal zazen will diminish your vital energy. Just practice reciting sutras with your mind in a settled state. That is proper training." {p. 252}

Worldly thoughts

In an evening talk, the Master said: "I always say that when chanting Noh you should make use of the energy of zazen. Do you think this is true?"

A monk replied: "Though I cannot do it, the reasoning makes sense to me."

The Master said: "You have no alternative but to strengthen your vital energy and, maintaining this energy, remove all worldly thoughts. That is all you can do. Your mind is always being defeated by worldly thoughts. You have to be quite careful about this." {p. 252}

Preparing tea

True monks

In response to a visitor who remarked that he couldn't discern the value of monkhood, the Master said: "Some think that monastic life is good and lay life is bad. From childhood they desire to be in charge of a temple. Seeking to achieve rank in the clerical hierarchy, they study the scriptures. They are no better than lay *pretas* in monk's clothing. Those who detach themselves from all of that and ponder Buddhism are true monks." {p. 252}

Nobody from a hundred years ago is around today

One day, in an emotional outburst, he said: "How idiotic! Nobody from a hundred years ago is around today. All traces of them have vanished. But, forgetting this, we desire trivial things and become planners and schemers. What stupidity!" {p. 255}

Be like a child playing in the rain and snow

One day the Master instructed someone: "I won't talk to you about the mind with which to practice religious austerities, but rather demonstrate the way to use your energy in daily life."

He then said: "No matter what you plan to do, act on the thought as it arises without deliberation. It's a mistake to think that you can act on it later on. The same applies to traveling. When the feeling to go somewhere arises, you should go. Don't think that you can do it later. Remember, for example, the feeling of your childhood, how you played in the rain and snow thinking, 'Ah, what fun!' When you can deal with everything in this nondiscriminating way, your mind will become exceedingly light." {p. 258}

Preparing tea

One day, watching the monks prepare tea in the tearoom at Tentokuin,[64] the Master thought that he should teach the youngsters how to prepare ceremonial tea. He went through the motions of preparing tea and said: "When you prepare the tea, remember: Don't delude yourself! Don't delude yourself!" {p. 261}

WARRIOR OF ZEN

Don't fritter your life away

On the seventeenth day of the fifth month of the Year of the Horse (1654), the Master gave instructions to Ichian[65]: "Practice until your mind becomes strong. Don't allow your energy to dwindle from constant study. It's meaningless to say, 'This wise man did this, this saint did that,' based on what you hear from others, and then walk around with your nose in the air. You will end up having contempt for people. I haven't seen even one person who achieved worth through scholarship. The more they study, the worse off they are. At any rate, if you keep on like this, you won't make it to thirty."

Someone then remarked: "Truly, scholarship is worthless! Take that Confucian so-and-so. Though he's studied extensively, they say he's become deeply immersed in greed."

The Master said: "He became deeply immersed in greed because his vital energy gradually began to wane. Without this unyielding vital energy, you can't tell how far to go. It's difficult to avoid attachments when your vital energy has waned. So, Ichian, whatever you do, don't fritter your life away!" {p. 265}

Premature satori

On the eighteenth of the same month, a layman said: "Having never heard any Buddhist teaching up to now, I feel quite ignorant." He then proceeded to ask about the essentials of Buddhism.

The Master said: "Be that as it may, you are fortunate not to have heard anything about the Buddha Dharma. Had you heard something, it might have led to a premature satori, followed by a feeling of freedom. But Buddhism is not something one simply hears and grasps. It requires practice in which you rid the mind of impurities little by little. Practice brings light to a mind in darkness and strengthens a weak mind. Let understanding of this be your first priority." {p. 265}

I'm still not free

One day at dawn, the Master said: "Though the great matter has penetrated my body and I feel myself to be one with it, I am still not free.

Those ancients who were said to have completed their religious training must have practiced with tremendous vigor!" {p. 267}

Repay a debt

During a meal, the Master said: "Having come into this world, I'd like at least to give back benefit equal to that I've squandered while here."

An elder who was present remarked: "We can't be expected to give back even a third of it."

The Master replied: "Oh, yes, we can! There are workers who do. Farmers, in particular, provide for this world. Many of them die, carrying the burdens of this world on their backs. I, too, would like to become a farmer and repay my debt. How important this is! How important!" {p. 268}

Don't be deluded!

One evening, a monk said: "Recently my practice has lost some of its vitality."

The Master said: "That's something I know nothing about. I've just pushed on with all the strength I could muster as the opportunity demanded. Finally, in my sixties, the meaning of the phrase, 'Don't be deluded' came to me unexpectedly. At that time I just danced about, saying, 'Don't be deluded! Don't be deluded!' My heart filled with gratitude. If someone had actually been about to cut off my head, I would have considered it an illusion. But I carefully thought it all through and returned to my old self and to my various methods of practice. I still can't stop treasuring this bag of dung. The thing that we call existence is deeply ingrained." {p. 270}

The determination manifest in Buddhist images

One day the Master said: "You should learn to practice in the midst of things. You have to learn to make use of your practice when eating, speaking, and carrying out all kinds of activities without growing slack. As your mind matures, your practice will become one with these activities. This is called attending to everything within your practice. If you don't train yourself with the determination manifest in Buddhist images, your practice will be no use to you. I've heard that the main image in Unsen in the province of Hizen[66] is the Four-Faced Bodhisattva.[67] It is an expression of one's complete energy being applied in all directions. The Eleven-Headed Kannon[68] manifests this same mind. The quiet repose of the *Tathagata* also embodies this vital energy, complete in every way. Generally, when we move in a particular direction, our vital energy focuses solely in that direction, leaving other directions unattended. I believe my understanding of the Fierce Deity of the Three Treasures[69] is complete, but I have yet to understand the Four-Faced Bodhisattva. I can't force my vital energy to operate behind me.

"The main image at Iwadosan Unganji in the province of Higo[70] is a Four-Faced Bodhisattva. I'm sure I once paid homage to this deity." {p. 270}

* * *

Shōsan likes to impress upon his students the difficulty and rarity of complete enlightenment. It is with this purpose in mind that he seems to use the symbolism of the many-headed Buddhas and bodhisattvas. They see in all directions while ordinary people see only in one or two or, as Shōsan says about himself, three directions. This is another example of Shōsan warning his students of the danger of making too much of a small insight.

I have procured the seed

On the third day of the tenth month of the Year of the Horse (1654), the Master instructed a dying monk: "Even though you die, it's not important. Nothing would change if you were to live to practice another twenty or thirty years. Though I have lived to the age of eighty, I haven't changed. But I have procured the seed.[71] You, too, should tell yourself that you won't lose the seed, and guard it to the end. Whatever lies ahead for you, even hell, just go to it. Whatever your body becomes, just be that. What happens to you isn't important. Everyone, including myself, throughout his many appearances in this world, has to keep from losing this seed. In the past, the Buddha Shakyamuni alone attained liberation. The other patriarchs, in particular the great teachers like Dengyō and

Kōbō,[72] were still far from the Buddha's realm. So set your mind at ease. Even if you live but a little while longer, it won't make any difference. After all, life span is a matter of karma. And that's something beyond our grasp. But the seed is dependent on us. So fix your gaze firmly, let go of everything, and guard it to the end."

Hearing this, the sick monk's mind was set right as he passed away. {p. 271}

Right before your eyes

One day the Master said: "To learn to be always in a state of meditation means never to let your vital energy wane. You would never allow it to do so if it were certain that you were to die tomorrow. It wanes because you forget about death. Grit your teeth, fix your gaze, and observe your death at this moment. There is always a tendency to allow this energy to wane. So you have to feel it so strongly that it seems as if it's attacking you. Fearless energy comes from this. At this moment death is right before your eyes. It's not something you can afford to neglect." {p. 271}

I give rise to a thought as great as Mount Sumeru

One day the Master instructed a man who was practicing sinking zazen[73]: "Rather than doing something worthless, just learn about death. You don't need anything else. Force yourself to study death till your energy doesn't wane even in your sleep. How you treasure this thoroughly rotten body! Hot, cold, painful, itchy, it causes you nothing but suffering. Repeat to yourself what a disgusting, tormented body it is, and glaring intently, challenge your usual state of being. I may not seem to be doing this, but if you watch as I fix my energy, I'm always gritting my back teeth, fixing my gaze, and glaring ahead. I've been doing this since I was quite young. I say 'back teeth' for lack of a better way to express it. They aren't actually my back teeth, but rather the teeth between my back and front teeth. With this energy, I firmly grit my teeth, fix my gaze, and glare ahead. Hence, I call this 'watchful warrior zazen.' "

The Master became stern, as though working himself up, and declared: "When I invoked Hachiman[74] in this way, I received a staunch energy.[75] That's what I'm referring to. When I make use of this energy, thoughts naturally cease to hinder me. This is the nature of my zazen. The sort of zazen practiced throughout the country, in which you are told not to give rise to thoughts, quickly produces the thought, 'Don't give rise to thoughts.' I tried this kind of zazen. Some time ago, when the priest Ban'an was in Iwamura, I traveled there from Ishinotaira,[76] thinking I would make the journey without giving rise to a single thought. It was this fearless energy that allowed me to keep my thoughts in check. It's not that I never have sinking thoughts. But if I didn't arouse the great thought, I wouldn't be able to stop the many others. Although no-thought zazen is practiced everywhere, I practice thought-*arousing* zazen. I give rise to a thought as great as Mount Sumeru."[77] {p. 272}

Thinking the Way will manifest itself, I go on

One morning the Master said: "How revolting this body is! I'm fed up with it! Still, thinking the Way will manifest itself somehow, I go on like this." {p. 273}

What a filthy body!

One evening, when he came out to relieve himself, the Master struck his body and said: "Oh, what a filthy bag of dung! Especially when I defecate and urinate, I feel this to my marrow. What a filthy body! I feel repulsed. How meaningless it is!" At other times, he would sigh: "How meaningless it is! Awake or asleep, how utterly meaningless!" And when the monks and lay people were gathered around his bed,[78] he would infuse them with energy as he sat up and asked: "What's it all for? What's it all for?" {p. 273}

It just hasn't happened after all

Once at midnight, the Master said: "It just hasn't happened after all! Alas, I underwent these hardships for nothing! Soon I'll decay and just wait for the end." {p. 274}

Lazy monks

Once when the Master was upset by the narrow-mindedness of the monks and lay people, some monks came by. The Master turned to them and said: "I'd hoped that those who came here would have at least some understanding, but not one of them does. I especially don't want to see any lazy monks. You good-for-nothings, get out of here at once!" Saying this, he quickly sent them away. {p. 274}

Shōsan attended to his death more than thirty years ago

When the Master reached Kanda,[79] he noticed a small two-mat room alongside the main house. He said: "I've found a good place to die. I'll die here." He then went inside. Isai and Shōchi[80] were always in attendance.

A monk asked: "Master, the doctors have said that your pulse is poor. How do you feel?"

Laughing, the Master said: "Shōsan attended to his *own* death more than thirty years ago."[81] {pp. 275–276}

Shōsan will talk of nothing but death

One evening, looking at those around him, the Master said: "How powerful this 'existence' is! You're all thinking, 'Shōsan's still alive, he remains in this world.' You're concerned about my illness, and it seems to be draining your energy."

He added: "Guard this feeling of death with all your might! That's all I ever say. As long as Shōsan's alive, he will talk of nothing but death." {p. 276}

My discovery of the Buddha image

One day the Master said: "This time I was born in this world and will die without having served any purpose. Yet if there has been any merit in my life, it lies in my discovery of the Buddha image. This can surely be found in the Buddhist sutras. You should look for it later. But even if it's not in a sutra, practice in this way and you won't regret it." {p. 276}

Final instructions

Though at first the Master would not allow anyone to enter his room, he did permit visitors during his final week. At that time, a monk urged him to give instruction on the essential points of Dharma.

The Master glared at him and said: "What do you mean? Not having understood what I've said over the last thirty years, you ask this now?" After that, nobody asked for instruction.

The Master passed away peacefully, at the Hour of the Monkey[82] on the twenty-fifth day of the sixth month of the Year of the Ram (1655). {p. 276}

Mourning the Master

That evening in the sacred precincts of Tentokuin, the Master's funeral was held in accordance with tradition. Forty-four disciples surrounded the burning corpse throughout the night. There was a fragrance, but no stench, and only a trail of white smoke. On the third day, when the ashes were removed, the Master's bones were seen to be white as snow. The congregation of men and women divided the remains and performed the ceremonial rites. After being divided, the remains were deposited in Tentokuin and the three temples where the Master had lived.[83] The cool ashes were placed in a small jar and buried on the northern slope of Tentokuin. An oval tombstone was erected and inscribed with the four characters *Sekihei Oshō.*[84]

The Master was seventy-seven years old[85] when he died. From his youth, he questioned the meaning of life and death. He shaved his head at age forty-two and attained satori when he was in his sixties. His religious practice was exactly as has been stated in this record. During his more than thirty years of work for the benefit of the world, he saved countless numbers of people. Shōsan was the Master's name when he was a layman, and he retained this name when he became a monk. His family came from Kumano in the province of Ki.[86] He was born in the province of Mi.[87] He was the eldest son of the Suzuki branch of the Hozumi family. After the Suzukis moved to Mi, they became retainers of the Matsudaira clan, garnishing honors as samurai. Many generations passed from the time they became Matsudaira retainers till the Master's birth. After the Great Commander[88] united the country and the samurai were left with few duties to perform, the Master took the tonsure. He wrote *Banmin Tokuyū, Fumoto no Kusawake, Mōanjō, Ninin Bikuni,*[89] *Nenbutsu Zōshi,*[90] *Ha Kirishitan,* and *Inga Monogatari.*[91] These seven books shine throughout our country with the light of the Three Treasures. Written to save people of this world, they were expressions of the Master's cherished wish.

{*pp. 276–277*}

2

Talks and Letters on Traditional Zen Topics

Shōsan and the Ten Oxherding Pictures

The Ten Oxherding Pictures are a series of drawings accompanied by prose and verse that depict the stages of development in Zen practice. As expressions of the spirit of Zen training, they represent another human attempt to explain the unexplainable. There are sets of five, six, eight, and ten pictures, the most well known being K'uo-an's Ten Oxherding Pictures.[1]

The ox represents the "Mind," in the sense of original Mind or original nature. The pictures and words attempt to present the levels of understanding of this original Mind and its different manifestations. The oxherd represents the practitioner trying to grasp his original nature. The ox and the oxherd, two separate entities, gradually merge. The final picture shows the oxherd entering the marketplace, signifying that a Zen man living in the world, freely mingling with ordinary men, is the manifestation of true compassion—the bodhisattva.

Shōsan was particularly fond of these pictures. His practice of identifying with the Buddha through various forms of his images (Niō, Fudō, Bishamon, etc.) goes well with the study of the Ten Oxherding Pictures. The final picture, "Entering the Marketplace with Giving Hands," affirms Shōsan's conviction that Zen must come to the people, or in his words, "The World Dharma and the Buddha Dharma are one."

Shōsan must have found the Oxherding Pictures helpful when he admonished young, zealous aspirants who, having experienced minor "realizations," believed they had fully understood the teaching of the Buddha. Using these pictures as a kind of map, he could point out to them that they had only scratched the surface of Zen.

The Ten Oxherding Pictures below were created for this book. They are the vision of a modern artist, working within the framework prescribed by K'uo-an and some of his contemporaries about nine hundred years ago. There have been countless versions of this series throughout the history of Zen, among them two well-known modern interpretations printed in English-language books.[2] Shōsan had his own conception of the Ten Oxherding Pictures, and he expressed it in brush at least once as evidenced by his commentary below. Unfortunately, no version by Shōsan himself has been located. The only restriction placed on the artist of this series, other than that of following K'uo-an's sequence of pictures, was that changes be made in three of the pictures in accord with Shōsan's conception as expressed in his commentary.

In Shōsan's teaching, a life of meditation in action rather than a life of passive zazen was fundamental. Meeting the Mind (i.e., the ox) straight on rather than from behind, the change he makes in picture three, deals with that. Another important tenet of his, that one should never allow one's energy to wane, was doubtless Shōsan's reason for changing the fourth picture. And most essential to his philosophy, the need for the practitioner to mix with ordinary people, inspired the changes in the tenth picture. There is another quality, a playful quality, in these pictures that I feel is in accord with Shōsan's more subtle teaching. He expresses it when he urges his listeners: "Remember, for example, the feeling of your childhood, how you played in the rain and snow thinking, 'Ah, what fun!'"[3]

Searching for the Ox

Finding the Tracks

Seeing the Ox

Catching the Ox

牧牛

Caring for the Ox

騎牛
歸家

Riding the Ox Home

The Ox Forgotten, the Man Left Alone

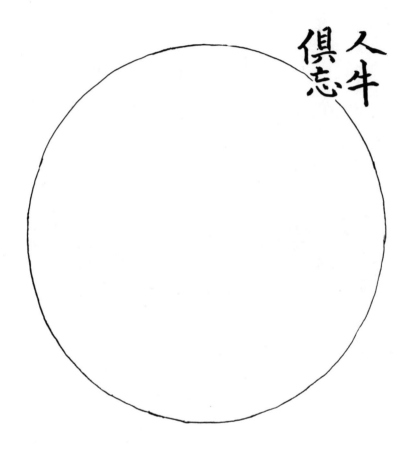

Both Man and Ox Out of Sight

Returning to the Origin, Back to the Source

Entering the Marketplace with Giving Hands

One day the Master said to the assembly: "The Oxherding Pictures are quite well done. But those who add their comments in praise of the work are making a mistake. The pictures were created largely because the teachers of that period[4] were always composing words and phrases. The pictures were designed to curtail this activity, and a method of practice in conjunction with these pictures was soon devised. However, people started adding their poems and comments to the pictures. Recently it has gotten to the point that whole books and poems are written and the pictures left out altogether. This is a great mistake."

In regard to this, a monk asked: "According to the commentary on the second Oxherding Picture, 'Finding the Tracks,' the oxherd realizes that, just as many different vessels are made of gold, all objective phenomena are projections of the self. But not yet distinguishing right from wrong, how can the oxherd know the true and the false?"

The Master said: "According to the sutras, 'Finding the Tracks' means that the aspirant practices until he sees that the many different vessels are all gold and that all objective phenomena become the self. But not being able to tell right from wrong, he still hasn't entered the gate. Provisionally, he is said to have 'seen the traces.'

"In the next picture, 'Seeing the Ox,' the oxherd sees his own nature. There are still people who can make this leap. However, the picture that follows, 'Catching the Ox,' is quite difficult. And the next one, 'Caring for the Ox,' is more difficult still. These two levels require exhaustive religious practice. In 'Riding the Ox Home,' you have to be able to make free use of your ripe mind. In 'The Ox Forgotten,' you are a man of no-Mind."

At that time, someone asked: "If the Mind is empty, how can the person remain?"

The Master said: "A person with an empty Mind can never be empty [so long as he has a body]. Though my nature was originally empty, this rotten thing called Shōsan is not empty. Coming this far means nothing."

Then someone asked: "The verse accompanying [the ninth Oxherding Picture], 'Returning to the Origin . . .' says:

Inside the hut he sees nothing outside,
Streams flow—whither no one knows,
Flowers turn red by themselves.

What does this mean?"

The Master said: "This fellow's mind is empty. When he sees something, there is only that thing. As for his appearance, he is nobody special: a man going to town with his gourd[5] hanging from his waist and returning home with his walking stick.

"You cannot complete the practice of these Ten Oxherding Pictures in one lifetime or two."

Once the Master said that it was a mistake to draw the ox from the back [in the third picture] and redrew it so that it was viewed from the front. He also drew the next picture, in which he had the oxherd pull the ox with great force. And in the tenth picture, 'Entering the Marketplace with Giving Hands,' he drew people in the market. He had the ten pictures made into scrolls, and his disciple Ikkei[6] had them printed and displayed. After that, he set out portraits of the Zen masters Mumon and Chūhō.[7] Above them, he wrote the character for *Mu*[8] along with his own motto. He hung the portraits to the left and right of the Ten Oxherding Pictures to show people the religious practice of the old masters. {pp. 212–213}

The Master summarized the Ten Oxherding Pictures: "The first picture, 'Searching for the Ox,' means the student sharpens his desire as he seeks the truth. In the second, 'Finding the Tracks,' he clarifies the teachings in the sutras and in the records of the ancients. A respectable man of knowledge can spit out words like one who has seen into his own nature. But a man of true vision will know true [enlightenment] from false.

"In the third picture, 'Seeing the Ox, 'the student realizes the Way through the sounds he hears, and understands the original Mind through the things he sees. All things are endowed with original nature. But this original Mind does not yet obey.

"In the fourth picture, 'Catching the Ox,' the student binds the ox-mind with a rope to make it obey him. This requires many years of religious practice. It's difficult for the ox to leave the field of delusion, and the student must understand this. Unless he follows this original Mind, the student will not escape evil. This is where practice becomes important. The student must exhaustively apply meritorious practices.

"In the fifth picture, 'Caring for the Ox,' though the ox mostly obeys the oxherd, it scampers off with the arising of a single thought. If the student relaxes his ox-mind, it will run amuck. He pulls firmly on the rope, entering a state of meditation. If the student doesn't apply rigorous religious practice constantly, you cannot call it [enlightenment].

"In the sixth picture, 'Riding the Ox Home,' the student, through his practice, becomes one with the ox-mind. He gives himself up to the ox-mind and no barriers remain. In the seventh picture, 'The Ox Forgotten, the Man Left Alone,' the student becomes a man of no Way. Though the person remains, the Way no longer exists. In the eighth picture, 'Both Man and Ox Out of Sight,' no Dharma and no trace of the student remain, as in the empty sky. In the ninth, 'Returning to the Origin, Back to the Source,' when the student, without an individual self, sees things, they are nothing but scenery. When he does anything, because he acts without self, there is only activity. That's why only scenery appears in the picture.

"The tenth picture, 'Entering the Marketplace with Giving Hands,' depicts a selfless person with outstretched hands. For him, delusion and enlightenment, the ignorant and the saintly, are all the same. Whatever he does, nothing obstructs him. Evil becomes good.[9] *Liquor stores and fish markets become places of conversion to Buddhahood.*"[10]

In connection with this, the Master said: "I didn't want to talk about good and evil with regard to the tenth picture, but I did so simply because of the phrase 'Liquor stores and fish markets become places of conversion to Buddhahood.'" {pp. 213–214}

Shōsan and the Zen Kōan

Kōans have been previously defined as paradoxical statements pointing to the ultimate truth (Introduction, note 36). But in their purest sense, kōans express the essence of Zen by cutting through excess verbal baggage to reach a truth beyond words.

The history of Zen is by and large a history of relationships between teachers and students, a history that abounds in such paradoxical statements. The old stories containing these words were later collected, anthologized, and used by teachers.

Shōsan, like other reformers of his time, became skeptical of kōans and seemed to employ them sparingly, if at all. In Roankyō, *however, he does discuss a number of traditional kōans and he sometimes found kōans useful to point out important aspects of Buddhism to his students.*

No difference between nirvana and samsāra

It is said in a sutra: *"The pure practitioner doesn't enter nirvana; the monk who breaks the precepts doesn't fall into hell."*[11]

The Master commented: "Splendid!" And added: "The pure practitioner is one who, detached from everything, goes beyond nirvana. The monk who breaks the precepts tramples both heaven and hell." *(p. 189)*

Hyakujō and the fox

In the story of Hyakujō and the fox,[12] the Master added his comment to the phrase "He does not fall into causation":

"Give birth to just one thought, and throughout eternity you won't escape the karma of birth and death."

He also added his comment to the phrase "He does not ignore causation":

"The tip of the tongue does not have bones."
    That evening Hyakujō ascended the rostrum in the hall and told the assembly what had happened with the old man and the story of causation. At which time Ōbaku said: "The old man made a mistake in his answer. As a result, he spent five hundred lifetimes as a fox. If he had answered correctly each time he was asked a question, what would have happened?

Shōsan's comment: "Embracing poison in great quantities."
Hyakujō said: "Come here, and I'll explain it to you."
Shōsan's comment: "The spirit of a crawling wild fox."
    The Master then said to the assembly: "If anybody asks me about this case [kōan] I would say: 'Do you know *this* Hyakujō?' and knock him down." *(p. 189)*

From the "Record of Ummon"

Ummon[13] instructed the assembly: "When the World-Honored One was born, he pointed to the sky with one hand, to the ground with the other, took seven steps, and said: 'In all the world I alone am revered.'[14] If I had been there then, I would have taken a stick, beaten him to a pulp, and fed him to a dog."

Shōsan said to the assembly: "Was this stick aimed at the Buddha? Who was it aimed at? Try to respond to this."
    One monk said: "It was aimed at those who don't know this mind is Buddha but are attached to the Buddha's outer form."

Another one said: "Since the Buddha is the destroyer of peace, it was aimed at him."

The Master said: "There are many who understand it that way and aim their sticks at the Buddha. Surely they should be punished. Ummon's instructions to the assembly were the great activity aimed at enlightening them. It was the same as Tanka's wooden Buddha[15] and Nansen's cutting the cat.[16] The important thing is what the assembly felt when he said: 'I would beat him to death with a stick and feed him to a dog.'" {p. 192}

Mumon's comment on Jōshū's Mu

Mumon said: "To understand Zen practice, you must pass through the barriers of the patriarchs. To attain wondrous enlightenment, you must completely stop the movement of the mind.

Unless you pass through the barriers and stop the mind, you will be like a ghost clinging to grasses and trees. . . ."

A monk said: "According to the ancients, the ghosts that cling to trees, not having penetrated the Way, will be reborn as insects that live off the trees' leaves. If these comments were true, people today would all have become insects, and there would be no people left. As I see people today, none of them has penetrated the barriers of the ancients. Why are they reborn as human beings?"

The Master responded: "The statement doesn't imply that people become ghosts clinging to trees and grasses in their next lives. All these people who don't stop the movement of the mind are ghosts clinging to trees and grasses *right now*. If they don't separate from everything and become completely independent, they will be persons clinging to this and that, all of them ghosts attached to trees." {p. 192}

On Fuke in the Record of Rinzai

It is said in the *Record of Rinzai:* "When you meet a man who has deeply penetrated the Way, in the first place don't try to advance toward it."[17]

A monk asked: "Does this mean that you don't stop anywhere?"

The Master said: "If that were so, you would be better off not follow-ing the Buddha Way, wouldn't you? Those words were not referring to a level of practice. As you function today, what could be lacking? It is from that place that those words were spoken."

In connection with this, he said: "After being transformed by the spirit of the priest Fuke, I was able to understand the meaning of those words. I may not reach the place where the Buddha dwells, but I have resolved to reach Fuke's place in this or a future lifetime." {p. 196}

> One day Rinzai and the elders Kayō and Mokuto were sitting around the fire pit in the monks' hall when Rinzai said: "Every day Fuke is in the streets acting like a madman. I don't know whether he is an ordinary man or a sage."
>
> Before he finished talking, Fuke entered and joined the group. Rinzai asked: "Are you an ordinary man or a sage?"
>
> Fuke said: "You say whether I am an ordinary man or a sage."
>
> Rinzai shouted.
>
> Fuke pointed his finger and said: "Kayō is a new bride. Mokuto is a Zen granny. And Rinzai is a bothersome young child, but he is equipped with a discerning eye."[18]

A monk asked: "Did these three elders actually have their discern-ing eyes opened?"

The Master said: "If we see them with Fuke's eye, all three of them are blind. Their levels of understanding were quite different. Wasn't Fuke's manner of pointing it out to them skillful?" {p. 197}

From the Record of Rinzai *on the mysterious mind*

> An ancient said: "The mind turns in accord with all situations; this turning is truly mysterious. If you recognize your nature in accord with the flow, there is no more joy and no more sorrow."[19]

A monk asked: "Does 'recognizing your nature in accord with the flow' mean that because of your instant awareness of this nature, when someone strikes you, you will naturally feel no anger; and when you want something, you will naturally feel no desire to take it from another?"

The Master said: "No, it does not. 'Recognizing your nature in accord with the flow' means that if you want, you take; and if you are slapped, just be slapped. If you follow the flow in this manner, [the mind] will turn in accord with all situations, with no limits. This is not instruction for the ordinary mind. It is for the mature mind. I may not be able to make you understand this subtle meaning." {pp. 196–197}

Miscellaneous Writings and Talks

On the block of doubt

. . . The Master said: "As long as your mind has a block of doubt,[20] even though you fall into the evil worlds, you will eventually attain the Way in a future life if you hold on to the seed. If you don't ever awaken this mind, how will you discover your fundamental nature? I call it the mind of fearless energy. If you attain it, you will never lose the seed, whatever happens, and you will be free in all your dealings. When a practitioner who hasn't attained this mind is faced with a life-and-death situation, he will surely lose the seed." {p. 200}

Nothing for the demon to hold on to

The Master said: "If you create [the idea of] a Pure Land and your aim is to be saved by the vow of Amida, a demon will attach himself to you through that aim. Because doubt, like the great sky, has no subjective body, the demon has nothing to hold on to." {p. 201}

Trees and grasses never discuss people's good or bad points

A layman asked: "An old song says that it's good to live deep in the mountains because trees and grasses never discuss people's good and bad points. I've heard that this is an instructional song. Is it a worthy one?"

The Master said: "I'd just like to change one word."

The layman asked: "Which one is that?"

The Master replied: "It's deplorable to live in the mountains because trees and grasses never discuss people's good and bad points."[21] *(p. 208)*

Dōgen's poem

Someone asked: "Dōgen,[22] the abbot of Eiheiji, composed the following poem at Kitano (in Kyoto) on the evening of the fifteenth day of the eighth month: *This evening I see the autumn moon / I'd longed to see once more. / How can I sleep?* This lingering attachment to the moon doesn't suit a student of the Way, does it?"

The Master responded: "That's not the meaning of the poem. Because Dōgen has mastered the Way of poetry, he composes the poem according to that Way. It is proper in composing poems to express your feelings through the moon and flowers. You people think that in all situations you must say, 'Don't be deluded!' and 'Let go!'[23] throwing everything out." *(p. 208)*

You'll go where your mind leads

The Master said: "In Mikawa, some time ago, a lady asked a senior priest where she would go when she died. The priest was baffled by the question. Isn't that ridiculous? Most priests nowadays cannot even respond to something like this." The Master declared that this was due to such people's lack of understanding of the Dharma and proceeded to give his own response: "You'll go to the place you want to go. Whether it's heaven or hell, you'll go where your mind leads." *(p. 211)*

Shōsan's instructions on the Path of Action

The following is an excerpt from a letter to a nun named Shōsei.

"There are two ways of approaching the practice of Buddhism: through reason and through activity. The man of reason awakens to the fact that all mutable things are like dreams, bubbles, shadows, lightning, or dew, and concludes that originally there is nothing at all. The man of action lays siege to the body and mind, uprooting the 84,000 delusions. Cherishing the mind and body to any extent is cause for falling into hell.

"To lay siege to the body and mind, realize the path of liberation through detachment from the worldly, and fervently mount your attack:

"• Take charge of your mind as one riding a wild horse would keep watch over it day and night, never losing sight of its movements. If you are negligent, delusions will arise, and you will suffer the painful result of your evil karma.

"• Concentrate your mind, fix your gaze, grit your back teeth, observe life and death with a sense of urgency, and generate an awareness of imminent death.

"• Maintain the mind of one who throws himself into the midst of a thousand to ten thousand enemy horsemen.

"Practice in this manner and your mind will naturally mature; no longer feeling agitation, you will be able to use everything freely. Even artistic performances cannot be completed skillfully without the use of this mind. When it comes to military valor as well, without this mind, you will be unable to cross swords with others. And when entering society and endeavoring to speak out, without this mind, you will feel yourself restricted.

"Therefore, even one who chants the *nenbutsu* should do so with a mind that controls the disease of delusion, a mind that isn't concerned with thoughts. By using the *nenbutsu*, you keep constant pressure on the mind. This kind of *nenbutsu* is Buddhahood itself. The *nenbutsu* recited with the hope of being born into the Pure Land only increases your karma in the world of transmigration. One who recites in this manner is merely seeking death. If you understand this reasoning, and always keep fierce pressure on your body and mind, watching them day and night and never forgetting to attend to them, you are to be called a person of tranquillity, a person with a robust mind, a secure person and a liberated person, one who has triumphed. Where are life and death for someone like this? Where is delusion? When you attain this mind, delusion is wisdom, and life and death are nirvana. In the face of satori, good and bad become good. In the face of delusion, good and bad become bad. It's truly regrettable that samurai do not learn about this free and unobstructed robust mind.

"I hope to have this read with care to the lords Gorozaemon and Rokudayū.[24] Even if they are averse to hearing it, they should still listen. . . .

". . . You too should not dismiss these things, but should carefully take their meaning to heart." {pp. 220–223}

Shōsan's Buddhism and the Secular World

For Shōsan, the virtue of Buddhism lay in its usefulness to his country and its people. Though he left the secular world and his military career for the life of a recluse, he soon realized that his calling was to a more active life. Shōsan's sense of mission, his dedication to bringing true Buddhism to people from every segment of society, intensified as he grew older. He considered the current state of Buddhism in Japan degenerate, and a signal manifestation of this degeneracy was the fact that Buddhism was generally believed to be of no use to the secular world.

The strength of Shōsan's Buddhism reveals itself in the dynamic way he confronts questioners and addresses assemblies of followers. Yet after years of teaching and campaigning for a new Buddhism that would touch the hearts of all Japanese, he realized that he had hardly made any impression on the established religious or secular leadership. Toward the end of his life, he placed his hopes in his writings, believing that through them his ideas for reform might be adopted after he was gone.

One of Shōsan's cherished notions was that a government edict, whose content he never actually spelled out, would help to realize "true" Buddhism in Japan. In the writings that follow, along with his call for a government edict, Shōsan discusses his views on the kind of practice he believed necessary to give Buddhism value in the secular world, and on his hopes for Buddhism in the future.

Five points in Buddhist practice

One day the Master said to the assembly: "Nowadays, methods of applying Buddhist practice are very poor. As a result, everyone says that Buddhism is of no use in the secular world. This is not so. The main point of what I refer to as 'Society's Three Jewels' is Buddhism's usefulness to society. Were it not, I would be wrong to call it that. In order to make people aware of its magnificent meritorious function, I wrote the *Meritorious Use of the Three Holy Treasures.*"[25]

In connection with this, the Master said: "Buddhist practice means subjugation of the six rebellious delusions. This cannot be done with a weak mind. With a firm Dharma-kāya mind,[26] you send forth the soldier of pure faith. And with the sword of the original void, you sever delusions, self-attachment, and greed, wholeheartedly making advances throughout the day. Provided you dwell in this diamond mind, applying it even in sleep, it will ripen thoroughly. You will no longer discriminate between inner and outer, and you will fully rout the karmic-generated knowledge-ridden demon soldier. Suddenly you will wake from your dream, destroying the citadel of reality. You will cut down the enemy, birth and death, and residing in the capital of wisdom, protect the peace. This diamond mind is the jewel that functions when a warrior displays valor. . . .

"A second point is that Buddhist practice firmly upholds the precepts and does not act contrary to the teachings of the Buddhas and the patriarchs. It controls the tendency to twist things and corrupt them; therefore, the mind becomes virtuous. Clearly understanding the true Way and the false and transcending the true, you make special use of a meaning beyond discrimination,[27] saving all beings uprightly and with compassion. This Mind, the jewel that makes use of the laws of the realm,[28] practices justice and reason, yet transcends them, clearly distinguishing the true Way from the false. Simply entrust yourself to the manifestations of this Mind and all its actions will be in accordance with the law. . . .

"Third, in Buddhist practice you divorce yourself from personal views and refuse to distinguish between self and others, while making use of the six harmonies.[29] Arriving at the true Mind, you repay the four favors[30] from above and save ordinary beings in the three realms of existence[31] below.

"I wrote about this mind and called it 'the mind that makes correct use of the five relationships'[32] because people were saying that Buddhism did not include these relationships. Can you say that a Buddhism that discards the personal self attains a nondiscriminating mind, repays the four favors from above, and saves all ordinary beings from below fails to include the five Confucian relationships? All ordinary people, moreover, are considered the children of the Buddha. Confucianism, on the other hand, stops at the five relationships.

"As for the fourth point in Buddhist practice, you discard the mind that analyzes knowledge, free yourself from attachment to objects, and, arriving at a mind of selflessness, let things happen as they will without any personal intention to be free. This mind is the jewel used by all performing artists. Artists skilled in their trade should know this. Strategists in the art of combat, in particular, should be keenly aware of it.

"The fifth point in Buddhist practice is the destruction of evil passions. Here, the luxury-seeking mind, the flattery-seeking mind, greed, and the fame-and-profit-seeking mind all disappear. I wrote about this mind and called it 'the jewel used to pass through this life' because people today mistakenly think that Buddhism is of no use to society.

"Buddhism destroys all evil passions. Insofar as evil thoughts disappear, you will continue unobstructed on your journey through this world. People are carelessly extravagant. Thinking they deserve more, they become greedy and destroy themselves. Whether they are of high rank or low, their greediness destroys them. Wherever they go, they find it difficult to survive."

The Master spoke again: "Although I've written about these five stages, it means nothing. I wrote about them because I will die soon, and I wanted to have people understand these teachings thoroughly. But they cannot be applied in this way all at once. It takes many lifetimes of continual practice before you can understand them and make a true vow to apply them in your life. Don't think you will make full use of them in one lifetime or even two. Even though I have thoroughly understood these teachings and clearly grasped the seed, I'm still not able to use it freely.

You may discover gold, but if you don't actually take it from the ground, you can't make any use of it." {pp. 229–231}

Shōsan's deepest wishes regarding religious practice

One day someone asked the Master to explain his deepest wishes regarding religious practice. The Master listed the following items:

"• In a sermon, the Buddha stated that the Dharma is bestowed upon the ruler, ministers, devotees, and patrons. That's why I wrote that the true teachings of Buddhism cannot flourish without a directive from the government. Even if the Buddha were to appear in the world now, it would be difficult to establish the true teachings. With a government directive, however, the true teachings would immediately flourish. For this reason, even the Buddha said that the Dharma was bestowed upon the ruler and ministers. Ah! If through this government directive we received the true teachings of Buddhism, I would have fulfilled my deepest wish. For more than two hundred years now, the true Dharma has been extinct in our country. But alas, this was inevitable! I've longed to present this point [the need for an official directive] to the government.

"• The Buddha is infinite grace and perfection. If you practice without aiming at infinite grace, you are not a disciple of the Buddha. I hope that you will practice aiming at infinite grace, because practicing without making use of this grace is not Buddhism. Now, without the ripening of your fearless mind, you won't be able to make use of this infinite grace. Infinite grace can be used to the degree that your fearless mind has matured. That's why I hope you will practice with this aim in mind. Using this infinite grace involves detaching yourself from your ego.

"• The Jewels of the Buddha, the Dharma, and the Sangha[33] are revered as the Three Holy Treasures. Having received the Three Holy Treasures, if you fail to share them with the people—and fail to make them a treasure of our land—you cannot call yourself a monk. I hope that you will practice religious austerities and guard the Three Holy Treasures, because the true mind is the Buddha treasure, the vow is the Dharma treasure, and charity is the Sangha treasure. Without the Sangha treasure, you cannot establish the Buddha and Dharma treasures. So, for the peace of all people and the prosperity of our land, I hope that you will practice the true Way. This practice is none other than the one Way of complete grace and perfection.

"• The Buddha Dharma is the teaching of the attainment of Buddhahood. However, there is a right way and a wrong way of understanding Buddhahood. If you cannot distinguish between the right and wrong way, all paths become the wrong paths. My wish is that you focus on the attainment of Buddhahood, and practice knowing that from that standpoint there are very few differences. All the sects know of no way of opening the Mind other than through discrimination.[34] And opening the Mind is Buddhahood. So clearly recognizing these right and wrong views, practice [Buddhism].

"• The practice of the Buddha Way is a means of freeing yourself from the three worlds.[35] That's why a monk is called one who leaves the world. If you don't aim at freeing yourself from the three worlds, you are not a monk. I wish that you would practice with the aim of freeing yourself from the three worlds, because in practicing self-freedom, you will focus on being free of name and form. The practice of freeing yourself from the three worlds is the destruction of the mind.

"• According to the Buddha's words, 'One who fully enters society lacks little from the Buddha world.' This statement means that you can attain Buddhahood through the world's teaching. This is because the world's teaching is the Buddha Dharma. It is written in the Avatamsaka Sutra:[36] 'The Buddha Dharma is not different from the World Dharma. The World Dharma is not different from the Buddha Dharma.' Unless you proceed according to the principle that you can attain Buddhahood through the world's teaching, you are completely oblivious to the intention of the Buddha. In a discourse of the Buddha, it is said: 'Not practicing the Buddha Dharma as you are, in society, is not Buddhism.' That's why I wish that you would regard the law of the world as the law of the Buddha. . . .

"• Consider the way Buddhist statues are arranged. At the entrance gate stand the guardian deities; the twelve divine generals stand in the drawing room[37]; the sixteen virtuous gods,[38] the eight *Vidyaraja* deities,[39] the four heavenly kings, and the five great lords[40] stand side by side, each exhibiting his power, clad in armor, bearing dagger, sword, spear, and bow and arrow. If you practice without penetrating the meaning of these deities, you will find it difficult to control the six rebels of delusion. And if you are careless in your practice, you will not be able to understand their meaning. I hope that as you practice, you will focus on the Buddha images. By focusing on the Buddha images, I mean carefully grasping the nature of each image, receiving its energy, and practicing with it as your model. You won't be able to practice unless you understand what receiving this energy means. However, if you don't have a feeling for this, nobody can force it upon you. If you take this to be something that can be learned, you will make many errors in the future. You just have to be ready to receive it."

The Master then said: "Though I have struggled for eighty years, there hasn't been anyone who has listened. The time was not right, [and it won't be long] until I rot away. I'm sad that there isn't anyone now who sees [the truth]. Still, I've placed copies of this petition of mine in shrines and temples throughout the country. I've left them there for the future in the hope that someone will come along with a feeling for these teachings." {pp. 231–234}

Statue of Shōsan at Shingetsuin, a temple founded by Shōsan in Asuke.

Scroll of three Suzukis: Shōsan; Shōsan's brother Shigenari; and
Shōsan's son, Shigetoki, adopted by Shigenari. Property of the
Amakusa Christian museum.

Sekiheizan Onshinji monastery in Asuke, founded by Shōsan in 1624. Sekiheizan Onshinji is in present-day Toyota City.

Pages from a 1664 edition of the *Nininbikuni* (Two Nuns),
written by Shōsan in the 1630s.

Notes

Introduction

The principal sources used for this introduction are: Suzuki Tesshin, ed., *Suzuki Shōsan Dōnin Zenshū* [Complete Works of Suzuki Shōsan, Pilgrim] (Tokyo: Sankibo Busshorin, 1962); Fujioshi Jikai, ed., *Nihon no Zen Goroku*, vol.4: *Shōsan* (Tokyo: Kodansha, 1977); Winston L. King, *Death Was His Kōan* (Berkeley: Asian Humanities Press, 1986); Mizukami Tsutomu, *Ikkyū, Shōsan, Hakuin* (Tokyo: Chikuma Shobō, 1987).

1. *Roankyō, zenshū*, p. 171. *Roankyō.* is a collection of Shōsan's talks and notes about the Master compiled by his disciple Echū(1628–1703). Along with collecting material for two records of Shōsan's talks, *Roankyō* [Donkey-Saddle Bridge] and *Hogo shū* [Collected Scraps of Paper], Echū wrote a short biography, *Sekihei Dōnin Gyōkōki* [A Record of the Life and Practice of the Pilgrim Sekihei].

2. *Zazen*, literally, "seated Zen," is a term used for seated meditation according to Zen prescriptions.

3. Shingon is the Japanese school of Esoteric Buddhism transmitted to Japan by Kukai (774–835). The word *Shingon* is a Japanese translation of the Sanskrit *mantra* (secret word, mystical syllable).

Tendai was the most popular school of Buddhism during the Heian Period (794–1191). Its center at Mount Hiei was the training ground for the founders of both the Zen and Pure Land schools of Buddhism in Japan. The Tendai doctrine is based on the teachings of the Lotus Sutra. Tendai was transmitted to Japan by the monk Saichō (767–822) in 805.

4. Though the two major schools of Pure Land Buddhism, the Jōdo and the Jōdo Shin sects, differed in their interpretation of how to apply practice (the Jōdo

Shin Buddhists would object to the term *practice* altogether), they both appealed to the need for a religion in which one could be saved merely by simple faith.

5. Yang-chi Fang-hui (992–1049), a seventh-generation patriarch of Lin-chi Zen.

6. Lung-ya Chu-tun (835–923), a Tang Zen master.

7. Yūhō Yokoi, *Shōbōgenzō Zuimonki* (Tokyo: Sankibō Busshōrin, 1972), pp. 170–172. A record of informal talks given by the Zen Master Dogen. It is an important text for Sōtō monks today.

8. James H. Sanford, *Zen-man Ikkyū* (Chico: Scholars Press, 1981), p. 133.

9. After checking the records of the troop movements, Mizukami Tsutomu claims that Shōsan may never have gotten to Sekigahara in time for the battle. See *Ikkyū, Shōsan, Hakuin*, pp. 99–111.

10. Echū (1628–1703) became Shōsan's disciple in 1651, four years before the Master's death. Along with collecting material for two records of Shōsan's talks, *Roankyō* (Donkey-Saddle Bridge) and another collection of talks similar in nature to Roankyō titled *Hogo shū* (Collected Scraps of Paper), he wrote a short biography, *Sekihei Dōnin Gyōgōki* (A Record of the Life and Practice of the Pilgrim Sekihei), from which much of the material for this biographical sketch was taken.

11. Fugen Bodhisattva (Sanskrit: *Samantrabhadra*) The right-hand attendant of the Buddha. He is often shown seated on a white elephant.

12. *Roankyō, zenshū*, p. 170.

13. See Mizukami Tsutomu's *Ikkyū, Shōsan, Hakuin*, pp. 148–154.

14. Daigu Sōchiku (1586–1669) and Gudō Tōshoku (1577–1661). Two well-known Japanese Zen masters of the Myōshinji line of Rinzai Zen.

15. *Roankyō, zenshū*, p. 151.

16. *Zenshū*, p. 74

17. The title *Risshi* is a high monastic rank in several sects, including Tendai and Jōdo as well as Shingon.

18. *Roankyō, zenshū*, p. 242.

19. *Roankyō, zenshū*, pp. 177–178.

20. *Roankyō, zenshū*, p. 231.

21. All monks vow to take refuge in the Buddha, the teachings, and the assembly of monks, referred to as The Three Holy Treasures.

22. *Roankyō, zenshū*, p. 231.

23. *Roankyō, zenshū*, p. 232.

24. The Jōdo Shin, or True Pure Land sect is a popular school of Pure Land Buddhism that follows the teachings of Shinran. Its followers believe that a single recitation of the *nenbutsu*, performed with a pure heart, is sufficient to save one. They oppose the idea of religious practice because they feel that any attempt to save oneself is an indication that one's faith in the power of Amida's vow to save all sentient beings is not strong enough. This radical departure from other Buddhist teachings isolates them even from other Pure Land sects.

25. In feudal Japan, obedience to one's superior took precedence over all else, and when one's conscience would not allow one to obey an order, one had to be prepared to die. Shōsan accepted this tenet of feudal life and even asked students to be prepared to die in similar situations. Still, he must have been heartbroken at the loss of Shigenari.

26. *Roankyō, zenshū*, p. 168.

27. *Roankyō, zenshū*, p. 150.

28. *Hogo shū, zenshū*, p. 303.

29. *Roankyō, zenshū*, p. 141.

30. Quoted from Robert N. Bellah, *Tokugawa Religion* (New York: The Free Press, 1957), p. 92.

31. *Roankyō, zenshū*, p. 249.

32. *Roankyō, zenshū*, p. 241

33. *Roankyō, zenshū*, p. 241

34. *Roankyō, zenshū*, p. 165.

35. *Roankyō, zenshū*, p. 170

36. Kōans are paradoxical statements pointing to the ultimate truth. Traditional kōans are drawn from records of encounters between early Zen masters and their students.

37. See, for example, William Bodiford, "Early Japanese Sōtō Kōan Literature," *The Ten Directions* 13, no. 2 (Fall/Winter 1992), p. 25.

38. Shōsan seems to use the terms studying death (*shi ni narau*) and guarding death (*shi o mamoru*) interchangeably.

39. *Roankyō, zenshū*, p. 150.

40. See text, pp. 40–49. *Zenshū*, pp. 238–242.

Part 1: Unorthodox Zen

1. *Onryō*. Spirit of a departed person bent on obtaining vengeance. Shōsan uses this image as an example of the extraordinary energy one should direct toward the goal of conquering the self.

2. Page numbers at the end of each selection refer to Suzuki Tesshin, ed., *Suzuki Shōsan Dōnin Zenshū*. See Introduction, first note.

3. One of the epithets of the Buddha. For Shōsan, the image of the *Tathagata* represents deep repose, a state of meditation too advanced for beginners to understand. Shōsan feels that if one begins by practicing this type of introspective meditation, he will deceive himself by attaining false states of quietude. "Beginners," for Shōsan, included himself as well as everyone he met.

4. Fudō Myō-ō, A wrathful figure, a form of Dainichi Nyorai (Sanskrit: *Mahāvairocana-tathagata*), the Buddha who expounded Esoteric Buddhism. Fudō is par-

ticularly revered in Shingon Buddhism. It is said that he was incarnated as a slave in order to serve all beings, and that he took a vow to destroy all evil in the world. In his right hand he holds a sword to smite the wicked, and in his left, a lasso to catch and bind them. Behind him rises a mass of red flames. Like the *Niō*, he possesses the vital energy necessary to fight deluded thoughts.

5. The buoyant, floating, or rising mind (*fushin*). Later, Shōsan said he replaced this term with *fearless mind* (*yūmōshin*), thinking that "buoyant mind" could be misinterpreted as "casual mind." See *Roankyō, zenshū*, pp. 227–228.

6. *Vajra* (diamond) mind (J. *kongōshin*), a term that signifies the solidity of a bodhisattva's will to practice wisdom and compassion.

7. A certain lady who for twenty years supported a monk in his practice, feeding and sheltering him, asked a young girl she was caring for to embrace the monk and report back to her. When the old lady heard that the monk felt nothing upon being embraced, she kicked him out and burned the hut, saying he had wasted twenty years of his life. The kōan appears in *Shūmon Kattōshū* (The Traditional Tangled Wisteria Collection), Kajitani Sōnin, ed. (Tokyo: Hozōkan, 1982), pp. 342–344.

8. *Tokuyū* is short for *Banmin Tokuyū* (Meritorious Practice for All), a piece Shōsan wrote giving specific instructions to samurai, farmers, artisans, and merchants. *Kusawake* refers to *Fumoto no Kusawake* (Parting the Grasses at the Foot of the Mountain), a work offering particular advice to novice monks. See introduction, pp. 8, 13.

9. Arhat (J. *arakan*). One who is free from all craving and rebirth. In early Buddhism, the Buddha was called an arhat, but after the rise of Mahayana Buddhism, the term *arhat* was limited to the saints of Hinayāna Buddhism.

10. *Shiki*. Energy that is aroused when one is aware that death can come at any moment. When aroused, this energy allows one to conquer death.

11. A traditional form of Japanese theater, it is a combination of dance and dramatized recitation of poetry interspersed with prose. The form of recitation often resembles the style used in chanting sutras. Shōsan was very fond of Noh chanting, which was popular among warriors and nobles during his time.

12. The passage from *Shimin Nichiyō* the questioner refers to is as follows: "The ordinary mind has a buoyancy that conquers all and a weightiness that is always defeated. When the buoyant mind is functioning, you are entering the Buddha realm. When the weighty mind is functioning, you are entering hell. Through the power of your vow to seek enlightenment, guard this buoyant mind day and night!" (*Zenshū*, p. 66)

13. A text later incorporated into *Banmin Tokuyū*. See note 8, above.

14. Genkū (1133–1212) was his posthumous name. Hōnen was founder of the Japanese *Jōdo* (Pure Land) sect and teacher of the great Pure Land master, Shinran.

15. In feudal Japan, when a vassal's conscience dictated that he disobey his lord's command, it was customary for him to commit ritual suicide (*seppuku*). Renouncing one's position as a samurai could very easily be interpreted as an act of disloyalty. If one's lord was displeased with the decision, he might require the vassal to cut open his belly.

16. Under Tokugawa rule, only samurai were allowed to wear both long and short swords. Although this was a time of peace, samurai had the right and duty to draw their swords to protect the law of the land. Some, however, took this as a license to cut down innocent citizens at will.

17. The word translated here as *reveal*—*zange*—literally means "confession." I have used *reveal* in an attempt to give the sentence meaning in this context.

18. A Zen teacher of some notoriety according to this passage. Otherwise unknown.

19. Dharmakāya, the essence of the Buddha or the ultimate truth of the Buddha. This suggests that Mutoku had certified this monk as having had an enlightenment experience.

20. A collection of Buddhist tales and parables edited by Taira no Yasuyori in 1180. The story referred to tells how Indra, the Hindu god, changed himself into a demon and recited the lines "Everything is impermanent/This is the Dharma of birth and annihilation" to the future Buddha, Sessen Dōji. Realizing there must be two more lines to this verse, Sessen questioned the demon. The demon said that he would reveal them only in exchange for Sessen's life. Sessen agreed, and the demon recited them: "Birth and annihilation are annihilated / Quiet annihilation is joy." Upon hearing this, Sessen threw himself from a mountain in order to fulfill his part of the bargain. He was saved by Indra, who had been testing his resolve all along.

21. Sessen Dōji is the name attributed to Shakyamuni Buddha during a previous life when he was a bodhisattva practicing the Dharma; in Sanskrit Sessen Doji is called Himālaya Kumāra. See note 20, above.

22. The story was taken from the *Hōbutsu shū*; the verse attributed to Indra in this collection appears in the Lotus Sutra and Nirvana Sutra.

23. Fuke (P'u-hua in Chinese; d. 806) an eccentric monk, whose independent spirit earned him Shōsan's admiration. The Japanese Fuke sect, whose adherents are known as *Komuso* in Japan, claims him as their founder.

24. Kayō and Mokuto (Ho-yang and Mu-t'ung in Chinese). These two Zen men are known only in the story from the *Record of Rinzai* to which Shōsan is referring. See Asahina Sōgen, *Rinzairoku* (Tokyo: Iwanimi Shoten, 1966) p. 135.

25. Rinzai Gigen (Ch. Lin-chi I-hsuan, d. 866), a noted Tang Zen master and founder of the Chinese Lin-chi sect.

26. Perhaps Shōsan's way of warning against believing that the act of becoming a monk will make one "sane" (i.e., will change one).

27. Shōsan uses this expression, *Tokinokoe zazen*, to express the need for a practice that will hold up in the thick of one's regular activity.

28. One of Shōsan's chief disciples. Nothing is known about him other than the fact that he restored the Kannon Temple in Inada, Higashi Osaka, under Shōsan's name.

29. *Maku mōzō*, a popular Zen phrase that Shōsan often used.

30. "Hungry spirits" or "ghosts" (*gaki* in Japanese), the inhabitants of the *preta*-realm, one of the six realms where souls of living beings transmigrate.

31. Hell, the world of *preta*, and the world of beasts, the three lower regions where souls of living beings are said to transmigrate. The higher regions are the worlds of fighting demons, men, and gods.

32. The kōan is: "A monk asked Chao-chou [Chao-chou Ts'ung-shen, J. Jōshū Jūshin, 778–897, a Tang Zen master who, because of his spontaneity and creativity, was greatly quoted in Zen annals], 'Does a dog have Buddha-nature?' "Chao-chou replied, '*Mu*.'"

This is usually assigned as an initial kōan to practitioners. Many teachers ask students simply to recite *Mu* in a kind of mantric fashion until a breakthrough occurs. The student, in these cases, is told not to concern himself with the meaning of the dialogue. This approach is in accord with the type of practice Shōsan recommends to his students.

33. Ma-tsu Tao-i (J. Baso Dōitsu, 709–788), one of the great masters of Tang Zen.

34. Shōsan seems to be warning students to beware of weakened resolve in the face of bodily desires.

35. I.e., the *nenbutsu* (praise to Amida Buddha).

36. Sutra recitation has been a practice in Zen temples throughout Zen's history in Japan. It is said to yield merit and is not generally considered a means of attaining enlightenment.

37. That is, there aren't any true monks. *Shukke*, home-leaver, is a name for a monk. When used as a verb, it refers to ordination. A monk is one who has left his home and entered the home of the Buddha.

38. Present-day Gifu Prefecture.

39. The seventh case of the *Wu-men Kuan*:

"A monk asked Chao-chou (Jōshū in Japanese): 'I have just entered this monastery. Please give me instructions.'

"Chao-chou responded: 'Have you eaten your breakfast?'

"The monk replied: 'Yes.'

"Chao-chou said: 'Then wash your bowls.' The monk had a realization."

40. *Ichimai kishō* is a short exposition of Pure Land teachings composed by Hōnen, the founder of the *Jōdo* sect, in 1211. I have not been able to identify the *Nimai kishō* and *Sanmai kishō*, presumably other testaments attributed to Hōnen.

41. The present-day Kanagawa Prefecture. Sō is the Sinicized name for the province of Sagami.

42. A famous cave at the foot of Mount Fuji, known as a dwelling place of evil spirits.

43. This is an opening phrase in many Noh plays.

44. *Jūroku zenjin*, sixteen gods who vow to protect the keepers of the *Mahā-prajñāpāramitā-sūtra* (The Great Wisdom Sutra).

45. *Shitennō*, kings of the four quarters, protecting the four corners of the earth.

46. *Jūnijin*, the twelve divine generals who serve the Medicine Buddha. Each is a manifestation of one of the Medicine Buddha's twelve vows to save humankind from physical as well as spiritual tribulations. The "twelve branches" stand for the twelve two-hour periods of the day, each branch symbolizing one of the animal signs of the Chinese zodiac.

47. See Shōsan's *Fumoto no Kusawake*, chaps. 10 and 11. In chap. 10, *Shashin o mamorubeki koto* (The Necessity of Concentrating on Renunciation of the Body), Shōsan writes: "You should uphold the renunciation of the body" (*Zenshū*, p. 83). And in the opening section of chap. 11, *Jiko o wasurubekarazu koto* (The Necessity of Not Forgetting the Self), he observes: "As a cat catching a rat is one from head to tail, eyes unblinking, you should guard your self properly (*Zenshū*, p. 84)."

48. *Jitsuu*. According to Buddhism, things do not have a permanent existence. Man's fundamental error lies in his belief that manifestations of this world are un-' changing.

49. *Shiigi* (the four dignified manners). All human postures have been divided into these four positions, and monks and nuns are expected to behave with dignity in each.

50. A Mahayana sutra that was popular when Buddhism was transmitted to China from India. It expresses a simple approach to understanding the Buddha Dharma.

51. Present-day Saitama Prefecture.

52. Daie Sōkō (Ch. Ta-hui Tsung-kao, 1089–1163). A Chinese Zen master known as an advocate of kōan practice.

Hakusan Muiganra (Ch. Po-shan Yuan-lai, 1575–1630). A Chinese Zen master of the Ming dynasty.

53. *Vaisravana*, the god of treasure, one of the four guardian deities who, according to Indian mythology, protect people in the four corners of the world.

54. Two demons who are known basically for being trampled upon by *Bisha-monten*.

55. Mystic syllables considered to possess the essence of a sutra.

56. An Indian monk who, according to tradition, came to China in 520, and is regarded as the first patriarch of Chinese Zen. He is known for his nine years of

Notes

"wall gazing" at Shao-lin temple on Mount Sung (Sūzan). Like the fierce temple guardians so often referred to by Shōsan, Bodhidharma is usually portrayed with a penetrating glare.

57. When a lay Buddhist dies, a priest writes his new Buddhist name on a grave stupa (*tōba*), a wooden post representing a pagoda, and reads a prayer to protect him in his new world.

58. Judging from the context, this expression seems to refer to one who acts as if he were enlightened.

59. Unidentified. *Chōrō* (Elder) can indicate a full-fledged member of the priesthood, but in Zen it is sometimes used as a simple term of respect.

60. For Shōsan, the warrior who rids his mind of impurities and understands original emptiness can overcome distracting thoughts and deal with all situations. He becomes unborn-undying because he is no longer affected by external conditions. For Shōsan's ideas on the unborn-undying mind, see *Banmin Tokuyū, zenshū*, p. 65.

61. *Koku*, a unit of measure for sake and rice. (One *koku* of sake is equal to fifty to a hundred gallons, one *koku* of rice is equal to 5.119 bushels, or 9.827 cubic feet.) Samurai received land from the government that was measured by the *koku* of rice produced.

62. It is common for parishioners to entertain priests with liquor.

63. In Japan, meals and drinks were traditionally served on trays placed on the floor in front of guests.

64. A Sōtō Zen temple in Ushigome in Edo (Tokyo) that Shōsan often visited.

65. A disciple of Shōsan. Otherwise unknown.

66. Present-day Nagasaki Prefecture in Kyūshū.

67. *Shimen-bosatsu*, a statue of a bodhisattva with four faces, each facing in a different direction.

68. *Jūichimen Kannon*, a statue of the bodhisattva Avalokitesvara wearing a crown with ten small headlike decorations, each of them representing an Avalokitesvara.

69. Sambō-kōjin, a deity believed to bring together the Shintō and Buddhist faiths. He is popularly believed to reside in the hearths.

70. Present-day Kumamoto Prefecture in Kyūshū.

71. Shōsan often refers to "the seed." It seems to be for him a taste of enlightenment sufficient to develop the determination to keep practicing and bears some similarity to the Way-Seeking Mind (*Bodai shin*), or Mind aspiring to the highest wisdom, a concept Dōgen often refers to in his sermons.

72. Dengyō Daishi (767–822). The posthumous name of Saichō, founder of the Japanese Tendai sect. Saichō was a prolific writer and his collected works fill five volumes.

Kōbō Daishi (774–835). The posthumous name of Kūkai, founder of the Shingon sect. Kukai wrote many works on Buddhism and was an accomplished calligrapher.

73. *Shizumi zazen*, an expression Shōsan uses to contrast with his "buoyant zazen." The former is practiced with sinking energy and, is according to Shōsan, useless. The latter conquers all. Shōsan's expression "skeletal zazen" (J. *nukegara zazen*) is synonymous with "sinking zazen."

74. A bodhisattva commonly called the God of War. He is also considered a Shintō god.

75. *Suwatta Ki*, referring to an energy in the *tanden* (a point below the navel) that is both stable and ready to spring forth when necessary.

76. The name of the valley where Shōsan's hermitage Sekiheizan was located. See introduction, p. 10.

77. Shumi-sen, the central mountain in a world, rising in the center of that world according to Buddhist cosmology. Each of the four heavenly kings governs one of its four continents, and Indra's heaven is at its summit.

78. Apparently describing the period at the end of Shōsan's life, when the Master was weakened by age and his followers gathered around his bed for instruction.

79. A town in Edo, present-day Tokyo area, and the residence of one of Shōsan's younger brothers.

80. Two disciples close to Shōsan in his final days. Otherwise unknown.

81. Shōsan may be alluding either to the time when he was critically ill after severe practice in Chidori Mountain (see above, pages 37–38) or to his becoming a monk (dying to this world).

82. Approximately 3 to 5 P.M.

83. The Onshinji at Sekiheizan, the Jushunin in Yotsukawa in Edo, and the Ryoshinan near Tentokuin in Edo.

84. Head priest of Sekihei. Sekihei is the name given the retreat where Shōsan lived for six years. See Introduction, page 10.

85. All ages in the text are based on Japanese reckoning, which counts a person one year at birth. Shōsan would have been seventy-six according to Western calculations. It was not uncommon to round off one's age in this way in a society that respected old age.

86. Present-day Wakayama Prefecture.

87. Province of Mikawa. See Introduction, page 6.

88. Tokugawa Ieyasu. See Introduction, pages 6–7.

89. *Two Nuns*, written in the early 1630s, is a prose narrative about a woman who finds solace from the grief of the loss of her husband through contemplation of death. It has been suggested that Shōsan was inspired to write this piece after reading Ikkyū's most well-known prose work *Gaikotsu* (Skeletons).

90. *Nenbutsu Notes*, written in the early 1630s, is a dialogue created by Shōsan between a monk and a nun in which the monk teaches the nun about Buddhism and the *nenbutsu*.

91. *Tales of Cause and Effect*, a collection of stories illustrating the Buddhist law that every action has its result, and likewise every resultant action has its cause.

Part 2: Talks and Letters on Traditional Zen Topics

1. K'uo-an Shih-yuan (J. Kakuan Shien), a Chinese Zen master of the Lin-chi sect who lived around 1150, is author of the poems and introductory words that accompany his pictures.

2. See Tokuriki Tomikichirō's rendition in Paul Reps, *Zen Flesh, Zen Bones* (Rutland and Tokyo: Charles E. Tuttle Company, 1957, pp.138–155) and Gyokusei Jikihara's rendition in Philip Kapleau, *The Three Pillars of Zen* (Boston: Beacon Press, 1967, pp. 301–311).

3. See above, Part 1, page 72.

4. The Sung dynasty (960–1279).

5. In ancient China, gourds were used as wine bottles. They were also considered symbols of emptiness.

6. Unknown apart from this passage.

7. Mumon Ekai (Ch. Wu-men Hui-k'ai, 1183–1260). A Chinese Zen master and compiler of the *Wu-men kuan*, a popular Sung dynasty kōan collection.

Chūhō Myōhon (Ch. Chung-feng Ming-pen, 1263–1323). A noted recluse on Mount T'ien-mu in China. He is said to have advocated a blend of Pure Land teaching and Zen.

8. For 'Jōshū's *Mu*,' see Part 1, note 32.

9. A Mahayana Buddhist idea. While training, the student is forbidden to eat meat, drink liquor, and so forth. However, the enlightened person is believed to transcend the ordinary categories of good and evil. He or she is believed to act from the "absolute," which might require breaking the precepts for the sake of a greater good.

10. Quoted from K'uo-an's introductory words to the tenth Oxherding Picture.

11. A phrase from the *Saptasatikā-prajnapāramitā-sūtra*, a sutra that sets forth the doctrine that all things are *sūnyatā* (voidness or emptiness). In Echū's short biography of Shōsan, he relates a story in which the Master, in his early twenties, impresses some senior monks with his quick and penetrating response to this kōan. (I refer to this phrase as a kōan because it conforms to the definition above, though it may not be found in any of the kōan collections.)

12. Whenever the Zen master Pai-chang Huai-hai (J. Hyakujō Ekai, 720–814, a Tang Zen master who is known for establishing rules for Zen monks) spoke to the assembly of monks. An old man attended the lecture. One day he remained after the others left and told the master that he had been a head monk at the time of the Buddha Kāsypa. When asked whether an enlightened person can escape causation,

he had answered in the affirmative. For this error, he was turned into a fox and had remained one for the last five hundred lifetimes. He asked Pai-chang to tell him what the correct response should have been. Pai-chang said that an enlightened person does not ignore causation. Upon hearing this, the old man thanked the master and asked him to conduct a funeral for the fox on the mountain behind the temple. The following day, Pai-chang took the monks to the other side of the mountain and conducted a funeral for the dead fox.

That evening, when Pai-chang told the monks the story, his disciple Huang-po Hsi-yun (J. Ōbaku Kiun, d. 850?) asked what would have happened if the old man had not given the wrong answer. The master told him to come closer and he would tell him. Huang-po stepped closer and slapped the master. Pai-chang laughed aloud, clapped his hands, and said: "I thought a foreigner's beard is red, but I see it is a foreigner with a red beard.'" The story appears in the kōan collection *Wu-men kuan* (case 2).

13. Ummon Ban'en (Ch. Yun-men Wen-yen, 864–949), the most anthologized Zen master in the traditional kōan collections.

14. From the *Tsung-jung lu* (J. *Shōyōroku*), a kōan collection compiled by two Chinese Ts'ao-tung masters in 1223.

15. Tanka Tennen (Ch. Tan-hsia Tien-jon, 739–824), a contemporary of Nan-ch'uan (see below, note 16). He first studied with Ma-tsu Tao-i (J. Baso Dōitsu, 707?–786?) and then went to Shih-t'ou Hsi-ch'ien (Sekitō Kisen, 700–790) returning to Ma-tsu. After Ma-tsu's death he traveled to various temples. At a certain temple on a very cold night, he took a wooden Buddha from the platform and burned it to keep himself warm. When the priest of the temple reproached him for his audacity, he said: "I am going to take out the Buddha's bones." When the priest asked how he could get the Buddha's bones from wood, he responded: "If I can't, then I am not to blame for burning the wood." This story appears in the *Ch'uan-teng lu* (Record of the Transmission of the Lamp), a Sung dynasty collection of Zen biographies.

16. Nansen Fugan (Ch. Nan-ch'uan P'u-yuan, 748–834), a well-known Zen master, disciple of Ma-tsu and teacher of Chao-chou. The story Shōsan is referring to is found in the kōan collections *Wu-men kuan* (case 14) and *Pi-yen lu* (case 63). The *Pi-yen lu* is a Sung dynasty kōan collection compiled by the Sung Zen master Hsueh-tou Ch'ung-hsien (J. Setcho Jūken, 980–1052) and later commented on by the Sung Zen master Yuan-wu K'o-chin (J. Engo Kokugon, 1063–1135). For *Wu-men kuan* see above, note 7.

17. This quote is followed by others in the *Rinzairoku* that warn against self-conscious effort in order to grasp what is already one's birthright. Then Rinzai says: "What are you looking for . . . your ordinary mind is the Way." See Asahina Sōgen, ed., *Rinzairoku* (Tokyo: Iwanami Shoten, 1966), p. 75. For Rinzai, see Part 1, note 25. The *Rinzairoku* (Ch. *Lin-chi lu*) is a record of the life and teaching of the Zen master Rinzai and is used as a source for kōans.

18. *Rinzairoku,* p. 135.

19. *Rinzairoku,* p. 93.

20. For Shōsan, this "block of doubt," which the student is usually asked to cultivate in kōan practice, is also the awareness that death can come at any moment.

21. Shōsan was critical of monks who remained aloof from society. He saw a danger of the recluse deceiving himself, believing he is enlightened, and staying away from places where his delusion could be pointed out to him. He also believed in the Mahayana spirit of the monk returning to the marketplace (see the Ten Ox-herding Pictures, pages 85–94).

22. Referring to Dōgen Kigen, see Introduction, page 5. The poem cited here was composed in Dōgen's last year when he had gone to Kyoto to seek a cure for his illness. It is included in the *Sanshō Dōei-shū* (Anthology of Enlightenment Poems by the Patriarch of Sanshō), edited by Menzan Zuihō and published in 1747.

23. "Don't be deluded!" (J. *Maku mōzō*) and "Let go!" (J. *Hōge jaku*) are expressions found in a number of kōans (see, for example, *Ch'uan-teng lu*, vol. 8, for the former and *Pi-yen lu*, case 4, for the latter).

24. Two samurai who apparently frequented a nunnery run by Shōsan's disciple Shōsei. Otherwise unknown. Other than another letter to the nun Shōsei in the *Hogo shū, zenshū*, page 307, nothing is known about her either.

25. *Sanbō Tokuyū*, composed by Shōsan in 1650, was later included in his *Banmin Tokuyū*. In it Shōsan tries to show how the Three Holy Treasures, Buddha, Dharma, and Sangha, should become a part of one's daily life.

26. Absolute Buddha Mind, limited neither by time nor by space.

27. *Mugi no gi*, literally, "meaning of no meaning," a common Pure Land Buddhist expression that means to let go of your discriminating mind. It is the attitude sought by Pure Land followers when reciting the *nenbutsu*.

28. Referring to the *Shohatto*, laws and regulations governing life in feudal Japan.

29. *Rokuwagō*: (1) Harmony of the body—prostrating together; (2) Harmony of speech—chanting together; (3) Harmony of thought—sharing the faith-mind; (4) Harmony of precepts—sharing the precepts; (5) Harmony of view—sharing common views of emptiness; (6) Harmony of benefit from practicing together—sharing the fruits thereof.

30. *Shion*, a term that usually refers to indebtedness to parents, ordinary beings, rulers, and the three jewels.

31. *San'u*, the realms of existence: attachment, form, and formlessness.

32. *Goron no michi*, referring to the five relationships posited by Confucianism. Expressed in terms of the virtues governing each, they are justice between ruler and ruled, kindness between father and son, distinctions between husband and wife, order between young and old, and companionship between friends.

33. Sangha, the Buddhist order or community.

34. It is unclear whether Shōsan is criticizing the other sects for using discrimination or using them as authorities to show that one must discriminate between right and wrong views. The Japanese here seems ambiguous. What is clear from Shōsan's general point of view is that he wants his students to concentrate on Buddhahood rather than on sectarian distinctions. All sects, Shōsan believes, agree that Buddhahood is the ultimate goal of Buddhism.

35. *Sangai*, the same as the three realms of existence. See above, note 31.

36. *Kegon-gyo*, a voluminous sutra setting forth the practice of a bodhisattva. The sutra preaches the doctrine that all beings without distinction have Buddha-nature and that all phenomena are interdependent.

37. See above, Part 1, note 46.

38. Ibid. note 44.

39. Deities in Esoteric Buddhism. They have a furious appearance and are said to destroy all evil spirits on behalf of the Buddha *Mahāvairochana*.

40. The first five of the eight *Vidyaraja* deities.

Glossary

bodhisattva (*bosatsu* in Japanese) One who holds back from immediately becoming a Buddha in order to save all beings and who works with compassion for suffering beings. The highest ideal in Mahayana Buddhism.

Buddha-nature The capacity for becoming a Buddha, inherent in all sentient beings.

buoyant mind (*fushin* in Japanese) A term used by Shōsan to indicate a flexible mind that deals with all circumstances.

death-energy (*shiki* in Japanese) A term used by Shōsan for energy that is aroused when one is aware that death can come at any moment. When aroused, he maintains, this energy allows one to conquer death.

Dharma Reality, truth, the ultimate law. In Buddhism it refers to the Buddhist teachings or the Buddha Way and consequently synonymous with Buddha Dharma.

fearless mind (*yūmōshin* in Japanese) The fierce mind that is never disturbed even in the face of daunting odds. Shōsan used this expression to replace his "buoyant mind" (see above) because he felt that the term *buoyant mind* might be misinterpreted as "casual mind."

the great matter A term often used to point to the essential points of Zen. It is sometimes called "the great matter of life and death," some-

131

times "the great matter of enlightenment," and sometimes "the great matter of cause and effect."

Kannon (*Avalokitesvara* in Sanskrit) The *bodhisattva* of great compassion, mercy, love. He vows to save all beings. Kannon was originally a male, but in East Asia this bodhisattva is commonly regarded as a female.

karma Results of actions; cause and effect, as distinguished from fate.

kenshō Literally, "seeing into one's nature," *kenshō* is equivalent to enlightenment or satori. It is sometimes thought of as a glimpse into one's nature, usually as the result of solving a kōan (see below). According to the way the word is commonly used, one can have many *kenshō*s before one's enlightenment is truly complete.

ki An expression Shōsan refers to often. It can be translated as "vital energy," which, for Shōsan, is the core of Buddhist practice. True Buddhist practice, he says, is the act of keeping up this ki. One way of doing this, he asserts, is to be aware of the fact that you can die at any moment.

kōans Paradoxical stories pointing to the ultimate truth. Traditional kōans are drawn from records of encounters between early Zen masters and their students.

mu Literally, "no," "negation." It is Jōshū's response to a monk's question, "Does a dog have Buddha-nature?" This is usually assigned to a practitioner as an initial kōan. Many teachers ask students simply to recite *Mu* in a kind of mantric fashion until a breakthrough occurs. The student, in this case, is told not to concern himself with the meaning of the dialogue, an approach in accord with the type of practice Shōsan recommends.

nenbutsu The recitation of the name of Amida Buddha, the principal practice of the Pure Land schools.

Niō Two guardian deities who stand on either side of a temple's gates (see Introduction, page 3).

preta Hungry spirits or ghosts (*gaki* in Japanese), the inhabitants of the *preta*-realm, one of the six realms through which souls of living beings transmigrate.

Risshū (Ritsu sect) A school based upon the Mahayana *vinaya*, the teaching that the observance of the Mahayana precepts is the way to the attainment of Buddhahood.

satori Enlightenment, or awakening, it is sometimes synonymous with *kenshō* (see *kenshō*, above).

shi ni narau To study death. A term frequently used by Shōsan and often interchangeably with *shi o mamoru* (see *shi o mamoru*).

shi o mamoru To guard one's death. A term frequently used by Shōsan.

sinking zazen (*shizumi zazen* in Japanese) An expression Shōsan uses to contrast with his "buoyant zazen." The former is practiced with sinking energy and is, according to Shōsan, useless. The latter conquers all.

six rebellious delusions (*rokuzoku bonnō* in Japanese) Delusions that occur through the six senses: sight, hearing, smell, taste, touch, and consciousness.

six rebels (*rokuzoku* in Japanese) See *six rebellious delusions.*

six roots (*rokkon* in Japanese) See *six sites.*

six sites (*rokusho* in Japanese) Also called the *six roots,* they are the organs in which the six senses operate.

skeletal zazen (*nukegara zazen* in Japanese) Zazen devoid of true spirit; zazen in form only.

sutras Scriptures containing sermons attributed to the historical Buddha. Most were originally composed in Pali and Sanskrit, though some were written in Tibetan or Chinese.

Three Holy Treasures (*Sambō* in Japanese) The Buddha, the teachings, and the assembly of monks. All monks vow to take refuge in these.

vajra (diamond) mind (*kongōshin* in Japanese) The term signifies the solidity of a bodhisattva's will to practice wisdom and compassion.

vinaya (*ritsu* in Japanese) Discipline; usually referring to the Buddhist precepts.

zazen Literally, "seated Zen," a term used for seated meditation according to Zen prescriptions.

zen energy (*zen ki* in Japanese) The energy that is at the core of Zen practice; Zen potential.

LIBRARY
ST. LOUIS COMMUNITY COLLEGE
AT FLORISSANT VALLEY

KODANSHA GLOBE

International in scope, this series offers distinguished books that explore the lives, customs, and mindsets of peoples and cultures around the world.

THE GREAT GAME
The Struggle for Empire in Central Asia
Peter Hopkirk
1-56836-022-3
$15.00

SCENT
The Mysterious and Essential Powers of Smell
Annick Le Guérer
Translated by Richard Miller
1-56836-024-X
$13.00

TIGER IN THE BARBED WIRE
An American in Vietnam, 1952–1991
Howard R. Simpson
Foreword by Pierre Salinger
1-56836-025-8
$16.00

ZEN IN AMERICA
Five Teachers and the Search for an American Buddhism
Helen Tworkov
Foreword by Natalie Goldberg
New epilogue by the author
1-56836-030-4
$15.00

THE HEART OF THE SKY
Travels Among the Maya
Peter Canby
New introduction by the author on the Maya peasant rebellion
1-56836-026-6
$13.00

CONVERSING WITH THE PLANETS
How Science and Myth Invented the Cosmos
Anthony Aveni
1-56836-021-5
$14.00

SONS OF THE YELLOW EMPEROR
The History of the Chinese Diaspora
Lynn Pan
New introduction by the author
1-56836-032-0
$15.00

THE WORLD OF THE SHINING PRINCE
Court Life in Ancient Japan
Ivan Morris
Introduction by Barbara Ruch
1-56836-029-0
$15.00

BLOODTIES
Nature, Culture and the Hunt
Ted Kerasote
1-56836-027-4
$13.00

WE HAVE EATEN THE FOREST
The Story of a Montagnard Village in the Central Highlands of Vietnam
Georges Condominas
Translated by Adrienne Foulke
Introduction by Richard Critchfield
1-56836-023-1
$16.00

AS WE SAW THEM
The First Japanese Embassy to the United States
Masao Miyoshi
1-56836-028-2
$13.00

WARRIOR OF ZEN
The Diamond-hard Wisdom Mind of Suzuki Shôsan
Edited, translated and introduced by Arthur Braverman
1-56836-031-2
$10.00

To order, contact your local bookseller or call 1-800-788-6262 (mention code G1). For information on future titles, please contact the Kodansha Editorial Department at Kodansha America, Inc., 114 Fifth Avenue, New York, NY 10011.